SIDMOU

HISTORY

ACKNOWLEDGEMENTS

The SVA Publications Committee acknowledges the immense work required in the preparation and publication of the first edition in 1987.

Amendments and additions have been made for this edition. We are very grateful to the following: Julia Creeke, Elizabeth Cunliffe, Brian Golding, Beryl McIndoe, Andrew Rugg-Gunn, Ian Simpson and Bob Symes.

John Dowell
Chair, SVA Publications Group

All Rights Reserved
© 1987 Sidmouth Museum
Reprinted 1988
Revised 2000
Revised 2015
ISBN 978-0-9934814-0-6

CONTENTS

Cover: From the original Long Picture of Sidmouth in the Museum. It is 2.6m. long, composed of six sections drawn by Hubert Cornish from three angles and published July lst 1815 by John Wallis Jnr.

Front: Centre showing Wallis's Marine Library.

Back: Other sections to West and East.

FOREWORD
to the First Edition

This short history of Sidmouth was the brain-child of Dr. Gerald Gibbens, Curator of the Museum 1972-85. He put the idea to the Museum Committee which readily adopted it and guaranteed the money needed for publication. Gerald has not only contributed two of the ten sections but has also given invaluable advice on the choice of illustrations taken from the Museum collection. Without the diligent care of the Secretary Margaret Carter in typing and re-typing the scripts and keeping a check on them as they circulated, as well as making many worthwhile suggestions, this book would have taken much longer to produce.

It is inevitable that with nine contributors there would be some overlapping and repetition but unless such information was too obtrusive it has been left so that the reader may pick out any chapter to study on its own.

A special acknowledgement must go to the late Ronald Wilson who over many years had delved into the history of the seventeenth and eighteenth centuries. He generously passed over the fruit of those researches to Sarah Jones of Exeter University who has written the section on that period.

It would be impossible to write a history of Sidmouth without consulting the work of Peter Orlando Hutchinson, the Victorian antiquarian. A cartoon of him and a short note by Catherine Linehan are presented as an introduction to this book in which he is frequently referred to as P.O.H.

G.H.

FOREWORD
to the Second Edition

The committee thanks Bernard Clark for providing material which together with valuable contributions by Reg Lane have enabled Sheila Luxton and Rosalind Whitfield, assisted by Margaret Carter, to compile the new chapter 'Towards 2000'.

FOREWORD
to the Third Edition

It is very timely and important that a third edition of *Sidmouth: A History* should now be published. This book brings up to date various aspects of the town's growth and cultural development not previously covered. Some amendments have been made to the original text and many new photographs used throughout. It is a must read for all of us with a strong affection for Sidmouth and its history.

Dr Bob Symes OBE
Curator Emeritus, Sidmouth Museum

PREFACE

Sidmouth is fortunate in having its own historian and diarist. Peter Orlando Hutchinson (P.O.H.), son of a doctor, came here with his family in 1825. He was then aged 15 and he lived here until his death in 1897. His legacy was a five-volume manuscript History of Sidmouth beautifully illustrated, a five-volume diary for the years 1848-1894, and six volumes of delightful sketches covering an even longer period. He was a prolific writer of books, articles to journals and magazines, local books and guides and letters to newspapers.

He seems to have known everybody from the skilled artisans to the gentry in whose houses he was a frequent and welcome visitor.

Peter Orlando Hutchinson

THE LAND

Much of the beauty of Sidmouth is in its setting. The front is beautiful, largely because of the great red cliffs and as the characteristics of the rocks affect us more than we know, the story of Sidmouth begins here.

The top, CLAY-WITH-FLINTS, is composed of the insoluble debris of a great thickness of chalk with all its stones and fossils. It forms a plateau and is pervious to rain so that it does not itself get washed away or allow rivers to form. Minerals and plant foods have been leached away and little grows. Under natural conditions trees get a poor start so herbage is thin. For ancient men, movement over it was easy and they had little reason to descend to the thick and frightening woods. The roads, then and now, are straight, and bend almost only to avoid streams whose heads are cutting back into the plateau. For the farmer it is dreadful land. A Sidford farmer said that his plough was worn down as much by a day on the plateau as by a whole season in the valley. Nowadays afforestation is the way to get some income out of the top but even that is far from easy. On the occasions when one comes across a freshly-ploughed field it is a pleasure to find especially good fossils, bits of natural bog-iron in odd shapes and even the outline of a hut circle or burial which may not have been noticed before. (The Exeter Archaeological Society or Museum should be told at once, with careful map-reference).

GREENSAND. Below the flinty top is the greensand which weathers a pale buff here but varies in colour. It was deposited in the sea. Water can easily percolate through the sand so that plant foods have been washed out and it is hungry; even so it does support more than the plateau. Afforestation is successful and is so common that this layer looks dark almost all round the valley. Limehaters like rhododendron, heather and whorts grow well. It forms slopes at an angle of l in 3 – too steep for a road to go straight up. Thus roads all over the valley and almost all round the edge of Blackdown have a straight approach up the red soils at l in 7 or less, bending sharply at the base of the greensand, and with an opposing kink at the top.

The poor soil was not included in a lord's land and nearby villagers ran their sheep and geese on the waste. In many counties there used to be argument about where the common land of the moor began. Here it is extremely easy, for, all round the valley, the top of the good red soil cannot be confused with the rough land above. Here are the 'goyles', the ravines where streams begin. If heavy rain falls on the flint cap, too much just to sink through, it has to pour over the edge of the cap where there is a slight dip, giving a dramatic start to a stream. There are about a dozen around the valley, the most obvious being the origin of the Sid itself, 400 yards west of the Hare and Hounds Inn directly beside the road to Ottery St. Mary. The best of all, though not the biggest, is on a path near Blackbury Castle, grid 175.938. I was there when a cloudburst took place and all of Broad Down was an inch or two deep in water which poured past my feet and tipped over the lip of the goyle, falling vertically with little speed but great volume.

So to the MUDSTONE, the horrible but more accurate name for the Keuper marl. Recently many names have been abandoned by geologists in favour of more accurate ones as in all professions. Marl contains over 20% calcium carbonate, which is far more than in our red rocks. These break down into excellent soil but even so, given a new garden of virgin mudstone, it is best to dig a great deal of humus into it. The face of the red cliffs shows many places at which water is thrown out by impervious 'waterstones' and temporary streams come out of sloping fields, often making small depressions. There are man-made 'marlpits' too, all round the valley and Polwhele in his great history of 1793 wrote "Marl hath power to fructify the barrenest land". The red mudstone does not allow water to penetrate as easily as greensand so that the boundary between them is wet and is known as the Moor Ditch. The lower paths along which all men could walk freely became some of our present footpaths, especially on Salcombe Hill. The most important thing about the underground junction between the greensand and the mudstone is that it dips downward to the east. Underground water from the greensand thus flows to the east where it has eroded a series of large and charming combes such as Lincombe and Burscombe from East Hill, whereas the dry west-facing sides of East Hill and of Sidbury Hill and Salcombe Hill are almost ruler straight.

The Sid valley is only six miles long but the valley sides are so steep that a rainstorm can cause a flood in the town unbelievably quickly. In 1981 the Water Board did good work in flood prevention by aiding the spread of water in unpopulated areas, slowing its speed by ingenious weirs and deepening the river in town, even underneath the Waterloo Bridge.

Sidmouth has an unusual addition to the simple valley-shape. If one stands on the Front in the forenoon and looks westwards, High Peak appears to have a vertical brick wall. Picket Rock, which must obviously be very hard, is the same height and is of Otter Sandstone which makes up the whole cliff at Ladram and beyond. A walk from the foot of High Peak back towards Jacob's Ladder shows that this hard sandstone dips down to the east and disappears under the shingle, but it suddenly comes up again to make Chit rocks and the Chit promontory. This strange behaviour resulted from an upward force below Sidmouth probably before the greensand was laid down about 100 million years ago. The Otter Sandstone cracked upwards (a 'fault') along a line from Jacob's Ladder to Lower Woolbrook. The little hills of Sidmount and Nappy Peaslands came up and are repeated further north, to give a handsome variety. The Hanger cliff against which the Sid flows is obviously sandstone and there is a contrary crack only a few yards east of the Sid's mouth.

PUDDINGSTONE. Vancouver wrote in 1808. "Ascending the coarse and flinty sides of Salcombe Hill, its top is found to spread into a sheepdown of some extent, affording a short and sweet herbage but on which huge masses of conglomerated flints interrupt the operations of tillage in the adjacent enclosures". We call this 'Sidmouth Puddingstone' as it is so local. It is composed of sharp flints in a silcrete matrix. The stones impeded also the proposed racecourse, so ingenious gentlemen said to their wives, "My dear, we must have a Rockery: quite the rage". Nearly all the big stones were carted down and are found in many gardens: the greatest are in the grotto at Knowle, now part of the garden of Knowle Grange. They are listed but may possibly be viewed by permission from one of the flat-dwellers.

SALCOMBE STONE, CENOMANIAN LIMESTONE. If the reader stands on the Front and looks east, the red lower part thins downwards and the top of the cliffs at Dunscombe becomes white due to the presence of chalk. Beer is all chalk. The other end of the dip is at Seaton Hole at the west end of Seaton beach and is worth going to see.

Salcombe Regis Church 1835
from Nature on zinc by E. Vivian, pubd. by Day and Haghe, Lithographers to the King

Just beyond Salcombe Hill the lower part of the chalk is lithified to form the Cenomanian limestone which is strong enough to be building stone. If the reader goes into the West door of Exeter Cathedral and at once turns right, there is a little door ahead and immediately on its left, a fine example of Salcombe stone. Some of the stone does have softer areas – a great headache to masons. In the East window of St. Francis Church in Woolbrook it is the most lovely that the mason had ever handled. The Warm colour of the 'young' stone weathers to grey, best seen in Salcombe Regis Church, especially in the south wall of the chancel outside, and at Dunscombe Farm where the stone is now again being quarried for Exeter Cathedral. The Fabric Accounts, 1279-1326, give details of the finance, even a pennyworth of nails for horseshoes, but they do not record which one of the several exposures was being worked. They do however record the transport and cost. About half of the stone went by barge to the unidentified 'la Sege' and half by land via Newton and 'Blackdown'.

At Beer, four miles further, the 'freestone' – fossil-free and grainless – has been famous ever since Roman times. It can be compared with Salcombe Stone if one stands inside Exeter's west door again and looks up to the vaulting far way up the nave on the right. It is clearly seen that the warmer Salcombe stone was continued by the paler Beer stone after an interval in building.

(More information is readily available in Sidmouth Museum.)

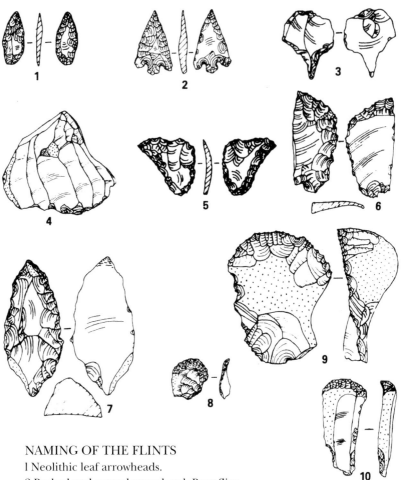

NAMING OF THE FLINTS
1 Neolithic leaf arrowheads.
2 Barbed and tanged arrowhead, Beer flint.
3 Piercers and borers.
4 Typical Neolithic core with long narrow flakes struck off.
5 Transverse late Neolithic arrowheads, *petit tranchet* derivatives.
6 Single-edged knife, Beer flint.
7 Fabricators; thick heavy-duty tools, all with much wear.
8 A typical "button" scraper.
9 & 10 Neolithic flake scrapers, typically with steep scraping angles.
Scale ½

By Sheila Pollard & Sheila Luxton,
reprinted by permission of the Devon Archaeological Society

THE PREHISTORIC AND ROMAN ERAS

The earliest signs of the occupation of the Sidmouth area date from about 3,300 B.C., the evidence being the collections from its hillsides of beautifully-worked flints from Muttersmoor assembled by Elsie Smith and from Salcombe Hill by Sheila Pollard, as well as many other finds in Sidmouth and around the valley, now in the Museums here and in Exeter. They were made from the local grey mottled flint or the glittering jet-black flint, much prized, from the prehistoric Beer Head site, the centre of stone axe production in the South-West. On Muttersmoor was an ancient circle of six stones, with one in the centre, to which the 'Seven Stones Lane' led from the Otterton road. In 1830 these stones were removed to be used in the rockery at Bicton.

The first known habitation was in early Neolithic times on High Peak, situated on the edge of the cliffs 2½ miles from Sidmouth front; it has mostly fallen into the sea and was probably six times the size of the present remnants. Excavations over several seasons, mainly during 1964 by Sheila Pollard, revealed blackened cooking areas, storage pits and flint tools, including a jadeite axe of Continental origin.

High Peak Earthworks
sketched by Peter Orlando Hutchinson, reprinted by permission of Devon Record Office.

There were no signs of later occupation in the Bronze and Iron Ages or during the Roman era, but the site was resettled in the Dark Ages after the Romans had left. A big ditch contained fragments of Mediterranean wine-jars and bones of ox and pig with a radio-carbon dating of c. 490 A.D. A surface-spread of charcoal may mean that the camp was finally burnt by the Saxons.

Shale cup from Broad Down,
Farway, East Devon

Food vessel, southern type.
Height 5 ins. Exeter Museum

reprinted by permission of Lady Fox

In the Bronze Age, (1500 B.C. onwards), a high 'flint-road' ran from Beer Head workings along the high ridgeways to the site of the present Hare and Hounds Inn, north of Sidbury, and on to Hembury or to Dartmoor. On the long ridgeway above Sidbury known as East Hill Strips are many flint cairns and rings containing grave pits. An extraordinary collection of burial mounds, usually known as barrows or tumuli grew up to the north and east of the Sid Valley, over fifty within a mile. The Victorians dug into these for treasure, but enough survived to show that the burials were all cremations. Daggers and various kinds of pottery were found including a small ornamental container holding the cremated bones of a baby: two holes in the pot signify the watchful eyes of the mother. The area contains the largest assembly of such barrows in Britain and is sometimes called the 'Farway Necropolis'. One tumulus can be easily seen two hundred yards from the 'Hare and Hounds' on the left of the road leading east.

Iron Age Camps
drawn by R. Lane

A	High Peak Fort	Si	Sidmouth
B	Belbury Castle	Ot	Ottery St. Mary
C	Hembury Fort	Aw	Awliscombe
D	Dumpdon Hill Fort	Ho	Honiton
E	Membury Castle	Gi	Gittisham
F	Musbury Castle	Ki	Kilmington
G	Hawkesdown Hill Fort	Co	Colyton
H	Blackbury Castle	Se	Seaton
I	Sidbury Castle	No	Northleigh
J	Woodbury Castle	So	Southleigh
Col	Colaton Raleigh	Sid	Sidbury

Hill Forts, often called 'Castles', mostly dating from the Iron Age, were occupied in Devon and Cornwall by the ancient tribe of the Dumnonii in the era before the Romans came. Around Sidmouth they form a double semi-circle: High Peak on the west starts the inner chain with subsidiary settlements on Bulverton and Core Hills; then Sidbury Castle, Blackbury Castle and Bury, ('Berry Camp') near Branscombe on the cliffs to the east. The outer ring begins at Woodbury Castle with its deep ramparts and the road over the Common actually cutting through it; then Belbury near West Hill, almost destroyed by forestry; Hembury, 'the great camp' and headquarters for the area since Neolithic times, standing nobly above Honiton, the only one in which much good exploratory work has been done; Dumpdon, the tree-crowned hill north of Honiton, and the three forts beyond the Axe, Membury, Musbury and Hawkesdown overlooking Axmouth.

These Castles were all fortified by the digging of deep surrounding ditches, a good refuge for men and beasts and well placed for watching a highway. Beautiful Sidbury Castle (300-200 B.C.), is on a projection eastward from East Hill; its entry took advantage of the narrow outlet westward to make strangers run the gauntlet. A very large cache of beach pebbles was found in 1862 by workmen during ploughing in front of the entrance; these were hoarded for use as sling stones in the event of attack.

In A.D. 50 the Romans established their headquarters at Exeter, called Isca by the Dumnonii, and it is thought that the mouth of the River Sid provided a small harbour and anchorage for them, as did the Rivers Otter and Axe. Roman coins have been found on Sidmouth beach and in other parts of the town, some bought from the fishermen by P. O. Hutchinson. In 1840 a remarkable bronze seven inches high was found on the beach about two hundred yards east of the river mouth; it shows the boy Achilles riding Cheiron the centaur hunting a wild beast, and probably helped to support a small tripod table or bowl. A good casting is in Sidmouth Museum.

The old coast road has not been proved to be Roman, but it runs in a fairly straight line between the river crossings at the Axe and Sid at Sidford; thence via Stowford, Greenway Lane and Bulverton to Newton Poppleford and on to Exeter. The 'lost' Roman staging post

Bronze Tripod Mount – Achilles riding Cheiron found in Sidmouth 1840

in East Devon called 'Moridunum' has not been identified but Hembury, Seaton and High Peak have all been suggested.

The only Roman buildings so far known in East Devon are Honeyditches on the western slope above Seaton and an interesting Romano-British villa above Lyme Regis. The excavations have been buried and turfed over but the finds included a fine Celtic mirror, a replica of which can be seen in the Museum, and thousands of local land and marine molluscs with a special spoon for eating them.

Many questions remain to be answered but archaeological exploration will continue to add to our knowledge of the Sidmouth area.

SAXON, VIKING & NORMAN TIMES

With the exception of the crypt in Sidbury church, not a stone of Saxon building is known in Devon except for some possible fragments in Exeter and some masonry at the base of the turret staircase of the tower of Branscombe church and in the tower itself.

Sidbury Church
drawn by H. Haseler, printed by C. Hullmandel

Sidbury was a nucleated village in Saxon times yet so far no occupational trace has been found in the area. Indeed very little Anglo-Saxon pottery up to and including the 7th century has been found west of a line from Bournemouth via Birmingham and Bradford to Bridlington. The significance of pottery is that it is indestructible and is usually the only trace to survive.

The Saxon occupation of the area began systematically in the early 7th century and there was some fighting. When, for instance, the Saxons advanced along the Roman road from west Dorset in 614 A.D.

they were met by a force of Britons who probably descended from their hill-fort at Hawkesdown where sling-stones have been discovered. A great battle was fought at Bindon on the downs above Axmouth and the British were defeated with the loss of over 2,000 men. The victors took over the fertile valleys of the Axe and Coly and perhaps pressed on as far as Ottery East Hill. Further fighting some forty odd years later enabled them to conquer Exeter and the rich red lands of the Exe and Culm valleys. However the occupation of East Devon and much of the rest of the county was most likely peaceful for there was plenty of land for the newcomers to occupy without taking over the farms of the Celtic Dumnonii scattered throughout the south-west. During the next four centuries, England became a land of villages and most of the names of those in Devon are of Anglo-Saxon origin. Sidbury and other local villages such as Axmouth and Colyton may have been colonised from the sea, perhaps during the latter part of the sixth century. The documentary evidence is very meagre, though it is known there was a monastery at Exeter c.680.

Danish invaders first reached Devon in 851 but were driven back. However, during the next 150 years they renewed their assaults at irregular intervals without attempting any permanent settlement. Exeter was attacked four times and on one of these occasions it was occupied for a whole winter before being relieved by King Alfred in 877, while in 1003 it was actually destroyed and plundered. It is known that villages near Exeter were burnt, so it is quite likely that other East Devon villages suffered. When raiding Danes seized lands belonging to Leofric, who was Bishop of Exeter from 1050 to 1072, Salcombe and Branscombe were among the possessions he recovered. In 1016 Devon and the rest of Wessex came under the Danish rule of King Canute. In all this time the Northmen made no settlements in Devon.

Before proceeding to the Norman Conquest, it should be noted that the mediaeval 'open-field' system with its individual and separated strips had its origin in Saxon times. Such strips are shown on the manorial map dated 1789 in Sidmouth Museum and indeed traces are still evident on the hillsides of the Sid Valley.

After the Danish raids came the Norman Conquest and in 1085, towards the end of his reign, William I ordered a great survey of his kingdom to be made. Detailed returns, sent to Winchester in 1086, were reduced to two volumes now known as the Domesday Book, Exchequer version. The original returns for the south-west are in Exeter Cathedral library and are called the Exon Domesday. In this volume Sidmouth is mentioned only in a marginal note under the Ottery St. Mary heading which starts in translation as follows: "The canons of St. Mary of Rouen have a manor called Otri (and one garden and one salt work which render thirty pence, in the land of St. Michael of Sidmouth) which they themselves had in the time of King Edward, and it paid geld for twenty-five hides".

Extract from Exon Domesday
reprinted by permission of the Dean and Chapter of Exeter Cathedral

There follows much detail, in archaic terms, regarding animals, land, and inhabitants. Geld was a tax and a hide a variable unit of land sufficient to support a household. It would appear that the monks at Rouen rented the garden and salt-pit from those at St. Michael's Mount in Normandy who were given Otterton and Sidmouth by William the Conqueror soon after the Conquest. Sidmouth was referred to in Domesday as Sedemuda. Up to 1066 Sidmouth had belonged to Countess Gytha, mother of King Harold, having previously been owned by successive kings. Most of the original large Saxon Devon villages were probably centres of royal estates. The salt-pit mentioned in the survey and perhaps the garden, would have lain close to the mouth of the Sid. Speaking of salt, various meanings of Salcombe have been suggested, the most likely being 'valley of salt'.

The Domesday entry for Salcombe translates as "Bishop Osbern has a manor called Selcoma, which Bishop Leofric held on the day on which King Edward was alive and dead, and it rendered geld for three hides. These can be ploughed by six ploughs. Of these the bishop has one hide and one plough in demesne; and the villeins have two hides and seven ploughs. There the bishop has sixteen villeins and seven bordars, and two serfs, and eighty sheep, and fourteen acres of wood, and six acres of meadow, and pasture one leuga long and four furlongs broad. This (Manor) is worth sixty shillings and when the bishop received it, it was worth as much".

The plough included the team of oxen drawing it. The demesne was the manor. Villeins were feudal bondsmen in different degrees of servitude: bordars were staff living on the manor and serfs were more or less slaves. A leuga is a league, a variable measure, but probably equal to the Roman league of 1.376 modern miles.

Thorn Farm, Salcombe Regis. Norman Stone Window
photograph by C. Hines

The manor house site is on Thorn Farm at the high north end of the village and there is a Norman stone window in the north gable.

At the road junction above the farm is a thorn tree in the middle marking the cultivation boundary, the common land being beyond it. It is thought that such a tree has been there from possibly before Saxon times. There seems to be no doubt that it was an early place of assembly.

Salcombe is nowadays called Salcombe Regis and the origin of 'Regis' is doubtful. It may have been acquired after King Athelstan gave the manor to the monastery in Exeter, or possibly when King Edward the Confessor took the manor back from Danish squatters in c.1050, but it was most likely added in the eighteenth century to distinguish it from the port of the same name in South Devon.

The Devon Domesday entry for Sidbury reads: "Bishop Osbern has a manor called Sideberia which Alvin and Godwin held in partage on the day on which King Edward was alive and dead and which rendered geld for three hides. These can be ploughed by twenty ploughs. Of them the bishop has one hide and two ploughs; and the villeins have two hides and eighteen ploughs. There the bishop has thirty two villeins and five bordars, and two serfs, and ten head of cattle, and three swine, and one hundred and forty sheep, and fourteen goats, and three hundred acres of wood, and twelve acres of meadow, and one hundred acres of pasture. It is worth six pounds, and when the bishop received it, it was worth as much".

The entry for Otterton to which Sidmouth became attached, begins: "The Abbot of St. Michael of the Mount has a manor called Otritona (and there is a market there on Sundays) which the Countess Gytha held on the day on which King Edward was alive and dead, and it rendered geld for fourteen hides ...". It is interesting that the details which follow include "thirty-three saltmakers".

As with the Saxons, there are not many traces of Norman architecture generally although nearly every mediaeval parish church existed by 1220. Later rebuilding has incorporated it or swept it away. Occasional Norman traces in plan form may be found in excavations or, more likely, Norman masonry in nave walls or a doorway or font. Salcombe church has a Norman circular pier in the north arcade and

Sidbury Church – East End Norman Decoration
photograph by Rev. J. Slessor c. 1865

the remains of a doorway in the south wall of the chancel: there are also small items of Norman ornament rearranged inside, as well as other features. Sidbury church has a complete Norman west tower and the body of the church is also Norman. The chequer-board decoration outside the east wall, and two windows, should be noted.

Archeology of the foundations indicates that there was a Norman church in Sidmouth. P. O. Hutchinson states that when the church was 'restored' in 1858-60 he saw "several interesting sculptured blocks of stone of Norman design".

It is known that many more places existed in Devon than are named in Domesday but they were mostly hamlets and single farmsteads. There were very few large settlements and in 1086 Exeter contained only 1500 people within its walls. Few towns existed in Devon in 1086: indeed by 1100 there were only four besides Exeter and they contained but three or four hundred inhabitants each. It seems likely, therefore, that the Sid valley was still very sparsely populated when the Normans imposed their power on Saxon England.

THE MIDDLE AGES

As a part of his distribution of the spoils of war, William the Conqueror gave the Manor of Otterton, including the Manor of Sidmouth which 'pertained' to it, to the Abbey of Mount St. Michael in Normandy. That grant was confirmed in a bull of Pope Alexander in the year 1178. Otterton Priory, however, was not endowed until the time of King John (1199-1216), who gave it the manors of Sidmouth, Otterton and Budleigh to enable four monks to celebrate Divine Worship and to distribute bread to the value of 16 shillings a week to the poor. The monks may have travelled over Peak Hill to the chapel of St. Peter in Sidmouth, and some stones of that chapel can still be seen in a wall of Dukes Hotel. Priory memoranda written in 1260 are preserved on the 49 vellum leaves of the Otterton Cartulary.

A section of the wall of St. Peter's Chapel which is mentioned in a deed of 1322 as an old and well-known landmark

The Manor of Sidmouth was managed by the Priors of Otterton for three centuries, and they received rents for land and farms, dues for corn and fish. They were particularly fond of porpoise, a delicacy at that time, and for each one they were prepared to pay the fishermen 12d, plus a white loaf to each man and two for the master. A deed of 1322 refers to the re-establishment of boundaries between the parishes of Sidmouth and Salcombe – the old ones had been confused by movements of the river. It speaks of a line drawn from St. Peter's Chapel tending Eastwards "versus portum" i.e. towards the port; it also mentions a cross near the chapel, probably Sidmouth's Market Cross. Early in the 13th century, Jordan of Tidwell near Budleigh Salterton exchanged the sheds, shops and stalls he had in Sidmouth's market with the Prior of Otterton, and the deed contains the first reference by name to the River Sid.

In those days, the town of Sidmouth probably consisted only of the portions around the Market Place, Western Town and the districts extending towards the river, and the 150 Sidmouth names or trades recorded in the Otterton Cartulary point towards a population of about 500 persons. As mentioned in the previous chapter, the Canons of St. Mary of Rouen held a manor called Ottery, and they rented one garden and one saltwork in the land of St. Michael of Sidmouth for 30d a year. That garden could have been used for growing vegetables, herbs and fruit to supplement a monotonous diet. Salt was valued as a preservative in the days before refrigeration, and was obtained from a pit with access to sea-water which was located in the Marsh – now drained and its seaward end called The Ham.

In 1336, in the course of warlike preparations against France, Edward III issued a writ to Sidmouth, with other ports along the south coast, for the supply of ships armed and manned to congregate off Portsmouth, but nothing came of it. Later, in readiness for the battle of Crecy, a further call for ships and men in 1346 brought a response from Sidmouth of 3 ships and 62 men. As Seaton sent 2 ships and 25 men and Exmouth 10 ships and 193 men we can judge the relative importance of the three towns. The war dragged on and in 1347 the siege of Calais produced another writ demanding money from coastal towns as far west as Mousehole in Cornwall. The king found it expedient to remind the reluctant and the rebellious that they could be thrown into prison to await the Royal Pleasure.

The river was gradually silting up and there was a general trend of flint or chisel eastwards along the Channel culminating in the great Chesil Bank. Various estuaries were becoming blocked as the rivers were driven over against their eastern banks; the Otter, the Sid and the Axe are each penned against eastern cliffs to-day. At that time Alicia Poale rented an area on the sand, perhaps for drying nets or sails, but it would not be possible to do so to-day. These long-term changes have contributed to the decline of Sidmouth as a port.

Various silver coins of the 13th century have been found on the land, in the river and in black sand at the base of the beach; they are evidence of trade at that time. However, most people had to work on the manorial farms, giving their labour – not necessarily willingly – for two or three days each week with additional duty at times of harvest. The names of Sidmouth's sub-manors are still familiar: Radway, Asherton, Bulverton, Woolbrook and Cotmaton. Probably related to the sub-manor of Cotmaton was the grant to Robert Bomore by Abbot Nicholas in 1267 of one virgate of land (some 30 acres) called "Bogemore" in the parish of Sidmouth. Doubtless Boughmore Lane is a relic of this.

The tenants were required to pay rents, typically 16d on 1st September which was the feast of St. Giles. In 1206 Henry Marshall, Bishop of Exeter, confirmed the gift of Sidmouth's parish church to the Abbot of Mont St. Michel. Manorial tenants were also subject to other dues such as Lambotte or Waxshott which were paid towards the cost of lights in the parish church, usually at 4d a year. The Otterton Cartulary notes that when the Abbot or Prior or any of their people should come, they were to have a white candle, salt, forage for their horses, and white or wood plates according to custom.

Corn had to be ground in the manor mills and these were vital to the prosperity of the neighbourhood. The monks of Otterton had set up a cross by their mill in Mill Lane, Sidmouth (now All Saints Road) the mill itself was located where Fords and Tesco now stand, opposite the Old Meeting House, which then lay at the northern edge of the town. The mill was on land belonging to Adam de Radway and was fed by a long gutter cut through from Lower Woolbrook and also by a stream down Mill Lane. Following a dispute, Adam gave up his claim in 1257 to the 'two mills under one roof' but it was accepted that he should grind his corn first when he arrived first as he had been accustomed to do. The monks won the right to dig turf to repair and keep up the banks of the mill stream where it flowed through Adam's land. The mill continued in use through the Middle Ages and was still in use until as late as the early 19th century when it fell into disrepair. It was eventually destroyed by fire caused by a drunken coachman.

Farming was probably on the 'open-field' system, originally introduced by the Saxons, for traces of it persisting until the 18th century enclosures are evidenced by a manorial map in Sidmouth Museum. It was a useful and practical arrangement whereby the lands of a settlement were divided into strips bounded not by hedges but by ploughing drainage channels. Each farmer could have strips of half to one acre in each of three or more large fields. This method gave a fairer distribution of good soil, poorly-drained land, moor and waste and also equalised the effect of leaving one field fallow for a season. Such a practice was economically sound when each man tried to grow enough to feed his own family, and the villagers had a shared interest in the development of the land even though it still belonged to the lord of the manor.

This peaceful rural life was disrupted by the spread from the continent, perhaps through Weymouth, of the bubonic plague or Black Death. One-third of the population of Devon is thought to have died; fields were left uncultivated, animals untended, and children abandoned parentless. Records of vicars in the local parishes show frequent changes taking place in the years 1348-50. The implication is that the incumbent died of the plague. This is not surprising, for a conscientious priest would have visited the sick, performed the last rites, and conducted the burial service. The contagious nature of the disease was not understood at that time. Changes occurred at all three of the local parish churches. In Sidmouth, Henry de Oustyn took over from Richard Todewell in 1349. At Sidbury Sir John de Creditone, inducted in 1348, lasted only a year before being replaced by Walter David; while in Salcombe Regis there were actually three changes with S. Rolle and P. Coombe being recorded for 1349 and S. Colytone for 1350.

The devastation caused by the Black Death forced a reorganization of agriculture for the scarcity of labour meant that fewer acres could be ploughed as arable, thus releasing pasture for sheep and cattle. More sheep produced more wool and the wool trade of Exeter expanded considerably: much of that wool must have been produced in East Devon and doubtless the Sid Valley played its part.

A royal writ closed many ports, including Sidmouth, to prevent the rich from decamping to Europe to escape the plague, taking with them their wealth, much of which then took the form of jewels, silver, money and other eminently portable valuables. Previously, the ports had been closed to prevent the infiltration of spies and seditious correspondence from France and all such closures must have caused losses of trade and of fishing, bringing further hardships. In these royal writs, Sidmouth was treated on equal terms with other ports in such matters as stopping the entry and exit of shipping, requests for nautical advice, and demands for ships manned for war.

Still the One Hundred Years' War with France rumbled on, although its battles concerned the nobility in the pay of the king rather than the common people. There was a royal confiscation in 1338 of English possessions of foreign religious houses including Otterton Priory; but for Sidmouth that merely meant the exchange of one remote landlord for another. That confiscation was a prelude to the great naval battle of Sluys and when victory had been won over the French, the manors were restored – but not until 23 years had passed. In 1360 a threat of invasion from France caused the king to order local ships to be drawn up high on land well away from the water. To the end of the century the kings continued to demand money for the pursuit of their wars against France.

By 1415 Henry V was on the throne and he laid the foundation stone of Syon Abbey at Isleworth in Middlesex. When the building was completed he endowed it with the Manor of Sidmouth among others previously belonging to French abbeys; thus Sidmouth remained under a distant landlord. In this same year Henry fought and won the battle of Agincourt. Parliament had recently granted the king one-fifteenth of the value of all 'movables'; and there were further taxes with a supplement of 'Benevolences' which were not always as voluntary as they should have been. All these impositions were to finance continuing battles in the domestic Wars of the Roses until in 1485 Richard of York was killed at Bosworth. In those wars between Lancaster and York, armies of a few thousand men fought each other in remote clashes between rival noblemen, but the mass of the population was never swept into a full-scale civil war and there is little to suggest that Sidmouth was much affected. St Giles Church was completely rebuilt around 1450 but there is no record of re-dedication. The tower, the north arcade, the 'five wounds window' and one of the bells are all that survive from this rebuilding.

The Court Leet of the Manor held in 1466-1467 listed various domestic misdemeanours, such as failing to repair ditches or to keep the highway clean. Other more serious offences named were the possession of daggers, knives and a bow and arrows which had been used for attempted murder and actual murder. Commercial infringements were charged against a miller for taking excessive tolls, a baker for baking and selling lightweight bread, and the 'forestallers' of fish brought to the harbour of Sidmouth. A common fault, complained of by the aletaster, was the illegal brewing of ales by many people who were obviously quite ready to pay the fine.

Throughout the 13th, 14th and 15th centuries life for ordinary men and women had been laborious with their houses uncomfortable and their diet coarse and monotonous. Yet their places in society had been secure, as was their unquestioning faith in immortality. Angevin, Plantagenet, Lancastrian and Yorkist kings had exacted contributions of ships, men and money for their foreign wars and the common people in Sidmouth as elsewhere had suffered grievously from foreign plagues. Resentful of taxation, ignorant of hygiene and fearful of disease they had nevertheless survived.

THE TUDOR ERA

A little over 100 years, but what changes they saw! A new dynasty established, the Pope rejected, the monasteries looted, a King with six wives (two beheaded!). Then came young Edward VI who favoured the Protestants, followed by Mary who, with Spanish backing, restored the power of the Pope, and finally Elizabeth who effected a compromise in the shape of the Church of England and smashed the might of Spain. What did it all mean to the small fishing town of Sidmouth, the tiny village of Salcombe Regis and the larger village of Sidbury with Sidford?

One King or another may have made little difference. Until 1540 Sidmouth remained under the care of the Abbey of Syon in Middlesex. This had its advantages because although Henry VII, a rather avaricious man, levied taxes frequently, he granted the Abbess a discharge of all manner of tolls and customs and stated that no goods or cattle of the said Abbess, nor of her tenants, should be taken by the purveyors, takers or buyers of the King's Household. The income from Sidmouth Manor in 1491 amounted to £44.9s.8d, in 1536 to £54.17s.7d and in 1540, when Henry VIII laid his hand on the monasteries, to £79.9s.2¼d. Even a farthing was still valuable!

When Henry VIII came to the throne in 1509 with a full coffer saved by his careful father he soon managed to run through it. For the first years, Henry was a very popular monarch – handsome, good at games and musical. Devon approved of him and many babies were named Harry. In 1523 war broke out with France, and Scotland was troublesome. Money was needed and the Commons granted the King 3s.0d in the £ on all income above £50 a year, with lower rates on those of lesser income and 4d a head from all poor people of 16 and over. To make sure what he could expect to receive the King had a general survey of the Kingdom made, with people's ages, professions, stock and revenue. In 1524 a preliminary levy for 23 names on the Hundred of Sidmouth Roll was taken at 2/- in the £ and included:

(1) William Welfare, Vicar of Sidmouth,   Tax 2s.8d
     on lands valued at £1.6s.8d
(2) Henneus Whyber, Edward Slade,   Tax 24s.0d
     John Pomeroy, on goods worth £12

(3) Thomas Purchase, on goods worth £11   Tax 22s.0d
(4) William Purchase, on goods worth £7.13s.4d   Tax 13s.4d
(5) Ambrosious Storch, on goods worth £5   Tax 10s.0d

Others were valued at £8 and £6 and lesser amounts. The names Slade, Pomeroy and Purchase still exist in the town: P.O.H. wrote in the 1850s that some of the richest men in the 1500s had descendants in his day who were shopkeepers and labourers.

A few months later, when another subsidy followed of 1s.0d in the £ on lands and tenements, 6d on goods, and 4d on wages, a long list of 108 names was made out for the parish, whereas the previous list was for the hundred. Thanks to figures given for lands and goods we learn something of the values of farming stock at Sidmouth in Henry VIII's time: one ox 20s.0d, one mare 20s.0d, one sheep 1s.0d. In 1538, when monastic establishments were tottering throughout the country, the Abbess Agnes Jordan granted a 99-year lease of the Manor of Sidmouth to Richard Gosnell for a yearly sum of £51.17s.7d and 40s.0d more to the stewards and bailiff. Two years later, the King laid his hand on the Abbey of Syon and confiscated the Manor of Sidmouth, among others, to his own use. The inmates of the House were dismissed with pensions. However, all these newly-acquired estates did not provide sufficient money for Henry who was now building forts and equipping a navy, so a demand was made to Parliament for further taxes. Sidmouth provided a 20% subsidy, levied at uncertain and unexpected periods. The valuation of Syon Abbey gives the valuation of Sidmouth in 1540 as:

Perquisites of Courts	£33.11s.0d
Rents of Assize	£24.17s.1½d
Other Rents	£3.15s.0¾d
Tenths of sheaves	£8.10s.0d
Farm of the Mill	£4.13s.4d
Works sold	12s.9d

In 1539 Sidmouth Vicarage was valued in the King's Books at £18.5s.5d. During the next six years, three further subsidies were levied; among the 156 names of those having to pay were Edward Slade and Thomas Purchase.

After the upheavals of Henry VIII's reign, when young Edward VI came to the throne, maybe Sidmouthians expected a little peace. The authority of the Abbess of Syon had been broken and spiritual teaching was in the hand of John Symys, vicar of the parish. He must have kept a low profile for he remained vicar under both Edward and Mary and into Elizabeth's reign. Perhaps the people of Sidmouth were likewise careful! Edward VI caused some disturbance in 1549 by bringing in the English Prayer Book using English instead of Latin and thus initiating the Prayer Book Rebellion. Catholics from Sampford Courtenay in mid-Devon were joined by others from Cornwall. They marched under a banner showing the five wounds of Christ and besieged Exeter for five weeks. A relieving force from London, composed mainly of foreign mercenaries and led by Lord Russell, was met by some of the rebels at Fenny Bridges and a bloody battle ensued. Within the course of the next few days further vicious fighting took place on Woodbury Common and at Clyst St. Mary before the rebels were crushed. All this occurred within a few miles of Sidmouth yet we do not know of anyone from the town being involved. Perhaps the influence of Rev. John Symys was too strong.

In 1549 it was obvious there was a great deal of distress among the population of the kingdom; all classes except those who benefited from the sale of monastic lands had become impoverished and the closing of the monasteries must have been a blow to the poor and ill who could no longer obtain food from them. Nevertheless a tax was imposed on goods and five Sidmouth names appear, four paying 10s.0d. each and one 8d.

After Edward died in 1553, Lady Jane Grey reigned for such a very short period – 9 days – that perhaps Sidmouth did not hear about her, and then Queen Mary came to the throne and restored Catholicism. The convent of Syon was re-established in 1555; the nuns were reinstated in their old quarters and granted endowments but there is nothing to show that the Manor of Sidmouth was given back to them.

For five years Mary reigned before being succeeded by her sister Elizabeth who was to remain on the throne much longer and become a legend through the ages. She, too, demanded subsidies and Parliament often grumbled as did the people who had to pay in the towns and villages. She however, discovered a new way of getting money: the law insisted that all people should attend their parish church, now Protestant again, and on those who would not, mainly the strong Catholic gentry, a fine of 12 pence per person was imposed. From a large household such fines should have brought in quite an amount of money but it was considered too small a sum to collect in some parts of the country. This was in the early years of Elizabeth's reign but about 1580 Lord Burghley, head of Elizabeth's government, brought in stricter laws. All who would not attend the parish church should pay £20 a month, with a fine of £100 for hearing Mass and possibly imprisonment.

Elizabeth did her best to keep out of wars which absorbed money, and played the 'marriage game' to keep France and Spain more or less friendly with her. Towards the end of her reign there was inflation, and the poorer people suffered. Subsidies were sought from 1589 to 1598 in the wake of the Armada and other troubles on the Continent.

One interesting name appears in a lease of 1560 for Tithes of Fish. Richard Gosnell's name is missing and John Leigh appears as the lessee and he leases to "Walter Ralegh the elder, squire, and Carowe Ralegh and Walter Ralegh the younger, all the tythe fish in Sidmouth commonly called the half-share, and also the tythe of larks." Young Walter would then have been eight years of age. They kept this tithe for eighteen years and then sold out for £60 to Sir William Peryam, who later became Chief Baron of the Exchequer. I wonder if Walter often came to Sidmouth from his home at Hayes Barton only five miles away and maybe heard wondrous tales from the fishermen! Sir William Peryam, John Scutt, yeoman, and others all had an interest in Sidmouth under the residue of the Gosnell 99-year lease.

What were Sidmouth, Sidbury and Sidford really like, and what sort of life was led in those far-off days? Sidmouth was said by Risdon in the early 17th century to be "one of the especialist fisher towns of the shire", trading with Newfoundland. There were occasional excitements! In 1586 the Channel was infested with pirates, and some foreign merchants and Sidmouth men subscribed £3.16s.8d and joined with men from Lyme in an expedition to capture them. Fairs were held in the Market Place on Easter Monday and Tuesday and the third Monday in September. The inhabitants would have had their feasts at

Christmas, Easter, May Day and harvest, enjoyed fairs and fairings, sung ballads sold by balladmongers, and heard tales told of Drake and Ralegh. They would have heard news of the Queen and perhaps exaggerated rumours of what went on at Court from visitors at inns or from packhorse men, and even pedlars or wayfarers. Roads were dreadful in both summer and winter, full of dust and potholes or mud. Even the Queen had trouble when travelling around the countryside on her many summer visits, though she never came as far as Devon. Births, deaths and marriages were always news, and sometimes the plague which struck in town and country alike. For medicines, people resorted to the wayside and garden herbs, or perhaps to a local 'wise woman' who could also give a fine love potion, or if she dealt in black magic could cast an evil spell on your enemy.

Sidmouth lost its harbour before Tudor times, and there has been much erosion of the coast since the 1600s. The cottages of the poorer

The mouth of the Sid in the early 1800s
by E.I.J. Esq., R. Ackermann's Lithographic Press, pubd. by J. Wallis 1819

fishermen have been washed away or, like those of the poorer farm workers, have perished long ago. There are a number of houses in the Sid valley which have external chimneys dating from the sixteenth century. Such a one is Tudor Cottage in Chapel Street, although soot blackening of the rafters over the hall, when the smoke from a central fire would have found its way out through a hole in the roof, suggests an earlier origin. Separated from the hall by a screen was the parlour with a chamber above. In 1972, when the place was being modernised, the screen became fully exposed and was carefully restored. Both sides showed paintings, the most striking of which was the royal arms of a Tudor sovereign, probably Edward VI. Merton Cottage next door would have been the domestic offices of what was then a substantial stone-built property belonging to the lord of the Manor. A frequent feature of the external chimney, as at Fortescue, was its siting in the roadside wall of a house as the proud sign of a prosperous farmer. There are some specially fine ones in School Street, Sidford.

There are other old houses in Sidmouth, one of which – Woolcombe House – is now the office of the Sidmouth Town Council. For some years it housed Sidmouth's Museum. It is much altered from its original state, but preserves part of its external chimney, and inside is a remarkable mediaeval hall, halved in height by the insertion of a floor. Manston Old House is certainly one of the oldest in the district still in use as a house. The chimney has a tablet with the date 1389 but it is doubtful if the date is contemporary though a former house may have stood on the site. A more likely date is 1589, and the house was probably a farmhouse. The most important surviving internal feature is the solar on the first floor at the south-east end of the house. The outer end wall has a good moulded chimney piece, and above, to the right, inserted in the wall, is an ornamental capital with head and leaf decoration. This is a 'green-man', a symbol of fertility illustrating pagan beliefs. All the wood used in the construction of the house was oak and no doubt locally grown; the original linenfold panelling is still to be seen.

There are Tudor cottages in Sidbury and Sidford, large and small. Some are of the long-house type, where the cattle were always on the downhill side of the owner's living quarters for obvious drainage reasons. There were other houses in Devon, where the cattle stayed downstairs and the farmer or cowherd went upstairs.

Screen in Tudor Cottage

Chimneys at Sidford, 1880
drawing by Peter Orlando Hutchinson, reprinted by permission of Devon Record Office

Interior of Woolcombe House, now Sidmouth Town Council Chamber

Manston Old House – sketch dated 1815

Farming must have been the chief employment in Sidford and Sidbury with fishing predominant in Sidmouth. There was certainly strip cultivation in the valley and sheep and cattle were kept. Ploughing would have been done by oxen. The wool trade was profitable and arable land was being turned into pasture throughout the 16th century. All the farmers had sheep, from 1,000 kept by the Wadhams at Chelson to smaller numbers kept by copyholders. As a result, farms were rebuilt to a higher standard of comfort. Most farm labourers lived in while others occupied rented cottages. The latter would almost certainly have included mariners and fishermen who, in their time on land, would have worked the strips near the sea just west of the parish church. Workers who lived in had board and lodging provided and wages were fixed in 1564 at £1 to £1.10s.0d a year for ordinary labourers according to age, while the bailiff or chief hind got £2. Women servants who lived in got 16s.0d to £1 a year according to age.

Of course there were other trades – Thomas Clarke, blacksmith, attended his daughter's burial in May 1596 according to parish records: there was a mill and a miller; there were certainly innkeepers. The Anchor Inn dates from 1840 but its foundations are reputedly Elizabethan; The Ship Inn, Old Fore Street, is said to date from 1350, and may once have been a church 'ale-house'. The drink was brewed by the wardens for celebrations and sold to the community for the 'ales' or town revels. Ale and cider were the favourite drinks of the poorer folk but until the reformation, when the church houses became redundant, brewing was not allowed to private individuals.

Food tended to be monotonous so herbs were widely used to give variety. Bread was made of rye or barley unless you were rich when you had white bread; beef and mutton were obtainable, or brawn and salted meat for the winter months because of the shortage of fresh meat. The poor had to be content with what they called "white meats" which included milk, butter, beans and fish. The eating of fish was made compulsory during Lent and on Fridays, by a law passed early in Elizabeth's reign, the object being to maintain seafaring and revive decaying coastal towns. It was repealed in 1585 but Sidmouth had plenty of fish. Larks and blackbirds were caught by netting, and "four and twenty blackbirds" were most likely part of a recipe for a pie! Rabbits or hares were available if you knew the farm bailiff or were a good poacher. The farmer lived well and the rich man exceedingly well with venison, chicken and swans on his menu. Parsnips, carrots, cabbage, artichokes, peas and beans were available and fruit such as apples, pears, cherries and plums. These could all be home-grown if one had a garden. Food prices rose as the century wore on and by 1572 prices for poultry were fixed at "best swan 6s.8d, stork 4s.0d, pelican 2s.0d, goose ls.2d, chicken 4d, larks per dozen 8d, blackbirds per dozen ls.0d, butter per lb.3d, best eggs 4 for 1d".

In 1588 a map was drawn, beginning at Sidmouth and going westward through Devon and Cornwall. It was part of a Government plan for fortifications on the coast against the Spaniards, but P.O.H. considered it was drawn as much by guess as by observation, so maybe it was just as well the Armada came soon after the project started so that the fortifications would not be built in the wrong places. To what extent, if any, the Armada could be seen from Sidmouth's hills is unknown but it seems likely that the Spaniards saw beacons in the area, for their Commander Medina Sidonia reported that "at dawn

Fire Beacon at Culmstock – photograph by G. H. Gibbens 1962

the Armada was near the land; so were seen therefrom whereupon they made fire and smokes". There is no reason to think that in this time of danger a fire should not have been lit in the stone beehive-shaped enclosure built on the spur at the south-western tip of Ottery East Hill, still known as Fire Beacon Hill.

Sidbury and Sidford deserve more mention. Sidbury was a nucleated Saxon village and Sidford a street village. The latter is now joined to Sidmouth by urban sprawl whereas Sidbury remains aloof. Most of the farms in the parish existed in mediaeval times. Many of the buildings in Sidbury village dating from the 16th century are of stone and cob under thatch and plaster. Buckley House is of many periods and is deemed to have been the hunting box of the Bishop of Exeter. Sand, still belonging to the Huyshe family, was rebuilt by Rowland Huyshe in 1594-1600 and is a good example of a late Tudor mansion It has recently been discovered that Sand Lodge is a late 15th century hall house. Sidford's ancient houses include Porch House (1574) and Warren Farm in Church Street. There has been a bridge in Sidford since the 12th century and the northern parapet of the present bridge is that of the old packhorse bridge.

Sidford Bridge – Pubd. by J. Wallis & H. Haseler, McQueen & Co., Lithographers

Salcombe Regis, like Sidbury, belonged to the Dean and Chapter at Exeter and the Dissolution did not affect it. The earliest will to survive is that of Matilda Harrys of Trow, 1547. In it she left her best sheep to the High Altar and her biggest brass pot and silk handkerchief to the head steward of the Manor. About this time Edward VI forced the Dean and Chapter to grant a 99-year ground lease to Sir Antony Harvey and affairs in the Manor were tightened up. The Crown took all Church ornaments except a silk cope and three bells and Sir Antony exacted higher rents. Moreover a new law required every farmer to keep a trained riding horse, the origin of the yeomanry. The tenants objected to all their new burdens and sent a round robin to the Cathedral but to no effect.

There was still much poverty in England as a whole and the 1601 Poor Law Act set up two overseers in every parish to see that employment was found for those in need, especially those who suffered from service in the army or navy whose children were to be apprenticed to some trade. The undeserving poor, those who would not work, were to be punished.

Looking through the records for Sidmouth Parish Church in the late 1500s, there is no mention of outbreaks of plague which could still be found in other parts of the country. A list of the numbers of baptisms, burials and marriages for 1599, 1600 and 1601 reads as follows:

	Baptisms	Burials	Marriages
1599	24	28	17
1600	12	10	14
1601	29	19	13

Elizabeth was dying, and the Tudor dynasty was nearly at an end. In 1603 James VI of Scotland and I of England came south with a horde of his followers eagerly awaiting the goodies they were sure would be theirs in England. The Stuarts had arrived. By the inhabitants of the Sid Valley as by the rest of the county, the change would doubtless have been regretted, for the reign of Elizabeth I had been enhanced by the deeds of many of the most famous men of Devon – Drake and Hawkins, Gilbert and Davis, Grenville and Ralegh. Only the last who, as we have seen, spent his childhood nearby, was to continue into the new reign but, sadly, to spend most of his surviving years in the Tower and then to end on the scaffold.

THE 17th & 18th CENTURIES

In 1603 at the accession of King James I, Sidmouth was a sleepy little fishing village much like any other, neglected beside the flourishing cathedral city of Exeter or the more substantial ports of Topsham and Salcombe. The sea had few of the pleasurable holiday connotations that it has for us to-day. Essentially it was, like agricultural land, a workaday commodity. As people sowed and ploughed in the one, so in the other they fished and traded. But by the end of the eighteenth century a new notion of the sea had entered the English vocabulary and what before had been treacherous coast now became treasured beach and Sidmouth, with its mild air and healthy waters, was converted into a thriving and popular seaside resort.

The manor of Sidmouth was in 1600 the property of the Crown. In 1604 the lease was taken by Christopher Mainwaring. He came from a junior branch of a prominent Cheshire family who, together with their cousins the Minshulls, had settled in Exeter. He held his first manorial court in 1605 when his tenants, yeomen who included names to be long associated with Sidmouth, such as the Harlewines, the Pearses, the Cawleys, the Channons and the Pynes, presented a forthright account of their rights. The Mainwaring family went on to buy the manor from the Crown but during the course of the 1620s it had changed once more and was by 1628 in the possession of the Prideaux family of Netherton who were to be the lords of the manor for the next 160 years. In 1610 Mainwaring had also disposed of the great tithes to Dorothy Wadham, co-founder with her husband Nicholas of the Oxford college that bears their name, intended for west country scholars.

Although Mainwaring relinquished his lordship in the 1620s, he and his family retained a connection with the parish for some years to come. Christopher's kinsman Randolph, who was vicar of Sidmouth from 1612 until his death in 1635, left in his will a sum of £5 for the churchwardens to distribute as loans to struggling fishermen and as late as 1729 those worthies were doling out l0s apiece to young Sidmouth men to help them to set up in the fishing trade. In 1635 John Minshull succeeded Randolph as vicar. A man it would seem of some learning, he had inherited Mainwaring's substantial library. By his will of 1663, Minshull left a generous benefaction for the education of poor children and the money raised went to found the first 'national school' in the parish. The schoolmaster received £5 per year at the school's inception. By the beginning of the nineteenth century 75 children every year were being educated under Dr. Bell's monitorial system then favoured in the county, although the schoolmaster's annual stipend had only increased to £10.

John Minshull's career as vicar spanned a period of dramatic national events: the Civil Wars, Commonwealth and Restoration. In 1644 Parliament issued an ordinance aimed, amongst other things, at discouraging the use of music in church services. The organ in Sidmouth church was removed, so that until the early nineteenth century the music in the church of St. Giles and St. Nicholas was provided instead by an orchestra. Hence there are a number of entries in the parish register for such unexpected items as "p'd. R. Stone 4s for strings for the bass viols". The incumbents of many parishes in Devon and elsewhere were ejected in the 1640s and 1650s for failure to conform to Commonwealth practice and there was a further round of evictions after the Restoration with the re-establishment of Anglican orthodoxy, but through all this Minshull survived unmolested, just as the parish as a whole seemed little affected by the great political events of the seventeenth century. Although, like the Vicar of Bray, he managed to accommodate himself to all the various changes in regime, Minshull did continue to enter baptisms in the parish register in defiance of an ordinance of 1653. Another law of 1650 which Minshull evidently acted upon was an act for suppressing incest, adultery and fornication for, in 1656, an unmarried mother from Sidmouth was presented at the quarter Sessions and ordered to the Bridewell or "house of correction" at St. Thomas's Exeter, while in 1659 a Sidmouth couple was presented by Minshull as "lewd and scandalous liveing people".

The Prideaux who bought the manor in the 1620s were an ancient family originally from Cornwall but long established in Devon as well. Sir Edmund Prideaux, who bought Sidmouth, was an eminent lawyer who had already purchased the manor of Netherton in the parish of Farway, a few miles north of Sidmouth, and Netherton remained the main seat of the family. During the early period of their Sidmouth lordship, its members were remarkably successful in maintaining and extending their wealth and influence.

In the Civil War of 1642, Sir Edmund's son, Peter, who succeeded in 1628, endeavoured to maintain a neutral posture that would not jeopardize his standing in the local community, but a younger son, John, raised a troop of horse during the Civil War, officered largely by men from Farway. At the same time Sir Peter's younger brother, named Edmund after his father, was an active partisan of the Parliamentarian cause in the 1640s and 1650s and served Oliver Cromwell as Attorney-General throughout the years of the Protectorate. In 1651, therefore, this younger brother had been in a position to apply with a clear conscience to purchase the various Crown lands in Devon that were then being sold off, acquiring the extremely desirable property of Forde Abbey and also Sidmouth Mills which had been retained by the Crown when the rest of the manor was sold to Mainwaring. This Edmund had died before the Restoration of 1660 and his son Edmund, although he lost the Cromwellian baronetcy, was nevertheless able to hold on to Forde Abbey and is said to have inherited a substantial fortune. The Royalist branch at Netherton was, of course, at the Restoration in high favour. Sir Peter had married his son, also Peter, to a daughter of the Royalist war-hero, Sir Bevil Grenvile and this son took his place in the Cavalier Parliament of 1661.

At the Restoration, Sidmouth Mills seem to have returned to the Crown and the lease was held as before by the Prideaux of Netherton, but it is doubtful if there had been any change of hands in practice between 1651 and 1660 when the Prideaux of Forde Abbey had held the mills. The purchase of 1651 was more probably by arrangement between the two brothers to ensure that the mills remained in the family and did not fall into the hands of outside speculators. (The interrogations by the Court of Exchequer in 1619, 1626 and 1672 show the value placed on the lord of Sidmouth manor's right that all customary tenants were obliged to use the manor mills). Divided loyalties within a family could be a tragedy, but it could also provide in uncertain times a form of insurance. Whichever side proved the victor, the Prideaux were unlikely to be the losers.

On Tuesday, 11th June, 1685, the Duke of Monmouth, an illegitimate son of Charles II, landed with a force of 82 men at Lyme Regis to remove James II from the throne and, with Parliament's blessing, to take his place. The three and a half thousand or more

A Mill near the Poor House
by E.I.J. Esq., R. Ackermann's Lithographic Press, Published by J. Wallis 1819

people who took part in this revolt included at least 730 Devonians with 14 from Sidmouth. The rebels were almost entirely common people and it was unusual that a gentleman from near Sidmouth should have been involved – a John Mitchell who is said to have fed rebel fugitives in the caves, possibly the underground quarries at Beer. Some help in the form of weapons also came from the Presbyterian Edmund Prideaux of Forde Abbey, mentioned above. Only four of the Sidmouth rebels' professions are known. They were from the cloth and craft trade, whose underemployment left them free to join the rebellion if they wished and to whom Monmouth offered freedom and an escape from poverty.

Monmouth's army was defeated at Sedgemoor in Somerset on 6th July. The rebels were tried and sentenced at the assizes held in September and October in Dorchester, Exeter, Taunton and Wells, conducted by five judges of whom today we remember only Lord Chief Justice Jeffreys. The one Sidmouth rebel to be hanged was Thomas Clapp, a comber, at Bridport on 12th September, and his land was forfeited. An alternative to hanging was transportation and courtiers with business interests in the West Indies bought prisoners for £10 a head. George Ebden and Robert Vauter, both woolcombers of Sidmouth, were transported to Barbados for Sir Jerome Nipho, the Queen's Italian secretary, though Vauter died at sea in December, and Matthew Eliott, a tailor, was sent for Sir Christopher Musgrave from Weymouth on the 'Jamaica Merchant' to Jamaica. John Mitchell was discharged for want of evidence and Edmund Prideaux, arrested after Sedgemoor and imprisoned in the Tower, was fined £15,000.

The handful of Sidmouth clothworkers who enlisted under Monmouth in 1685 is evidence of Sidmouth's involvement in Devon's important textile industry, though as manufacturers rather than prosperous merchants. In 1674, 'a Fulling Mill newly erected' was leased by Sir Edmund Prideaux to John West, a fuller of Sidmouth and in 1699 a clothier Samuel Pearce rented a plot of land for wool washing by the mill near the Red Lion. But by mid-eighteenth century the industry had ceased in Sidmouth and a manor deed of 1755 mentions 'a plot of ground, whereon the Tucking Mill stood, now a garden'.

The churchwardens' accounts and other parish records bear witness not only to the serious problems of pauperism and vagrancy persisting throughout the seventeenth and eighteenth centuries but also to the efforts made by the parish to alleviate the problem – relief paid to the sick, most often women of the parish, including those in childbed, as well as efforts made to apprentice the children of the poor to local merchants. Anomalies and curiosities there were, of course. A poor woman in childbed might expect financial relief when the child to be born was legitimate but an unmarried mother could only expect to be carried off to Exeter Bridewell, and payments for such transportation are as frequent in the records and as costly as the payments for relief. The records also give an interesting glimpse into the diversity of medical practice. The parish made contributions towards the upkeep of Mary Magdalene Hospital in Exeter and there are references in the accounts to payments made to doctors for their treatments. But it was an age when even the mathematician and philosopher Thomas Hobbes was said to have preferred the ministrations of a "wise woman" to those of learned physicians and as late as 1702, we find mention in the Sidmouth parish records of money paid to such a woman for curing a patient's eyes. Even in 1793 there were 60-80 paupers in Sidmouth out of a population of 400-500, and some £350 had to be collected each year to help finance the expenses of the parish workhouse.

It has been pointed out that Sidmouth was little affected by the Civil War of 1642-6. In fact the parish's coastal location meant that Sidmouth was more likely to lose men to the navy than to the army. In 1643 by order of the Quarter Sessions, the inhabitants of Sidmouth and Salcombe were specifically exempted from service on the 'posse comitatus', (a military obligation on all men between the ages of sixteen and sixty), on the grounds that they were busy enough dealing with the threat of enemy shipping "attending the coasts". There was also the constant fear of invasion from mainland Europe with which England was afflicted from the time of the Reformation until the period of the Napoleonic wars. The coast lying between Sidmouth and Seaton had been fortified to some extent since Tudor times but by 1627, when war with France gave rise to fears of invasion, the

View of Sidmouth Beach looking East featuring The Fort,
by E.I.J. Esq., R. Ackermann's Lithographic Press, pubd. by J. Wallis 1820

ordnance was found to be unserviceable. The following year French ships were so frequently in evidence off the coast that Sidmouth fishermen were afraid to put to sea and the Deputy Lieutenants of Devon asked the Earl of Bedford, then Lord Lieutenant of the county, to persuade the Privy Council that Sidmouth should have a fort of its own. Whether built then or somewhat later, Sidmouth did receive permission to erect a fort and there are occasional references to powder and shot being ordered for the ordnance there.

The naval wars against the Dutch in the late seventeenth century naturally brought some prominence to Sidmouth and other fishing ports as a recruiting-ground for sailors. Two Sidmouth widows were obliged to petition the justices of the peace for aid following the deaths of their husbands at sea. One Margaret Haycraft had lost her husband John on 28th May, 1665, "Shote through ye bowells" on board the frigate Dunkirk and she was left destitute with "three small sickly children". John Haycraft had been a pressed man but Robert Levermore of Sidmouth was a professional seaman, mortally wounded in the third Dutch war of 1672-3, leaving a widow Eleanor and three small children. The period from 1689 to 1815 was one of almost continual involvement in continental wars on a scale not known in England since mediaeval times. Sidmouth no longer retained immunity from its effects and we read of money being paid out by the churchwardens for maimed soldiers in 1703 and a further sum for quartering a wounded soldier six years later. By order of the parish authorities, Sidmouth was en fête in 1706 for the Duke of Marlborough's victory over the French at Ramillies.

Many more men from Sidmouth must have been lost in these years to naval service although some protection was granted to fishermen from the unwelcome attentions of the Topsham press-gang. Even this protection was removed at the end of the eighteenth century when the Sea Fencibles were formed – a sort of naval Home Guard composed of fishermen and boatmen and all "seafaring dwellers of the shore who were not liable for impressment". In 1794, when there was great alarm at rumours of a French invasion, Sidmouth raised 80 men for the Sea Fencibles who manned the battery at the Fort Field which, at this time, consisted of four twelve-pound guns and a six-pounder field-piece, and the signal station on Peak Hill. Measures were also taken to remove non-combatant inhabitants out of danger and to drive all cattle inland.

In 1630, Risdon wrote that Sidmouth was "one of the chiefest fischar towns of this shire". Fishing certainly was the main industry of the town, particularly associated with the Newfoundland cod-fishing, although still secondary in importance to the busy ports of Exeter and Topsham. Many local men fitted out ships for the long journey across to Newfoundland, maintaining their own plantations there, and a fleet of the smaller "bye-boats" that were used for the actual fishing. As early as 1600 there is record of a Sidmouth ship, the Charity, under its master Edward Cannon, making its way to the Newfoundland coast. The ships would set out as early in the year as the weather allowed, travelling via ports in Spain and Portugal where they would stock up with salt to preserve the fish, remaining in Newfoundland until the following autumn when they would return laden with salted fish and cod-liver oil. The boats carried most of the fish back to Spain and Portugal for sale to their Catholic population and returned to Devon with wine traded in exchange for the fish.

The most substantial Sidmouth family to be involved in the trade was the Folletts. Nonconformist tenant farmers on Sidmouth Manor, the Folletts really came to prominence in the middle of the eighteenth century when Samuel Follett established himself as a mercer, dealing in silks and woollens, and graduated to an interest in the fisheries. In the 1720s and '30s, his ship, the Ann, operated out of Topsham and he acquired the plantation of Trepassy on the Newfoundland coast. Two of his sons and a nephew Robert took their part in the trade and by the end of the century the Folletts were among the most prosperous tenants of the Sidmouth Manor, acquiring further landholdings, maintaining divers trading interests and operating a fleet of seven ships engaged in the fishery-trade. As the family became more prosperous, many of its members moved away from Sidmouth to take their place among the gentry of Salcombe and Topsham, but Samuel's grandson Abraham died in Sidmouth at the age of sixty-five, mercer, shopkeeper and gentleman-farmer and a pillar of the dissenting chapel.

It would be wrong to suppose that the prosperity that came the way of the Folletts was by any means widespread amongst the Sidmouth community. The majority of those involved as mariners in the Newfoundland trade simply hired out their services to shipowners and merchants. In the 1770s, one visitor to the town records that they "were for the most part in low circumstances", and this was the period when the trade was at its height. There was even the beginning of a shipbuilding industry with stocks on the site where the York Hotel and York Terrace now stand. The decline thereafter was dramatic and the firm of Follett in Sidmouth slumped rapidly. By 1787, only four ships from Devon made the journey across to Newfoundland, two from Topsham and two from Dartmouth. By 1820 the Topsham trade in Newfoundland had entirely gone and Sidmouth's own long involvement in the fishing there had come to an end. For the average mariner or fisherman, without his own land or other business interests to turn to, the situation must have been grim indeed.

There was a strong vein of religious nonconformity in the town as in most of south-east Devon, often associated with those engaged in the cloth trade. During the reign of Charles II a congregation of Presbyterians was formed. It is said that they met in an old barn that had two exits so that the congregation could escape through the inn

Sidmouth Old Meeting House & White Hart Inn
sketch by J. Comer

when a prosecuting official was on the warpath. The Declaration of Indulgence in 1672 tolerated nonconformist worship and since there were no chapels in Sidmouth, services took place in other licensed buildings. One was the house of Jane French in what is now East Street which in May 1672 was licensed as a Presbyterian and Independent meeting place. One of the ministers licensed in the late 1680s was Samuel Stoddon of Woodbury. He ministered to congregations at both Sidmouth and Sidbury and thought that the two should be combined. In his will of 1706 he stipulated that the Sidmouth house be sold and the money be used for a new building at Sidford. The Presbyterians of Sidmouth would not agree to this and, after much wrangling, Sidmouth's own chapel, now the Unitarian Chapel, was built in 1705 on the site of the old barn at the north entrance of the town, at the corner of Mill Lane (now All Saints Road). It shared the same thatched roof as the adjacent building which initially was the parsonage to the Chapel but later was converted into the White Hart Inn and tenants paid rent to the Chapel. (In 1886 All Saints Road was widened and the White Hart Inn was demolished).

There were further disagreements among the congregation of Sidmouth when some turned to Arianism, a belief in God as the Unity rather than the Trinity. These came to a head in 1719 when fifty-five ministers in the county agreed "to declare their faith in the Trinity" and thirteen refused and left the assembly. However, in the end, under the influence of Edmund Butcher, minister from 1798 to 1820, the Sidmouth church did become Unitarian.

Through the bond of nonconformity and the maritime interests in America that developed as a result of the Newfoundland trade, the parish forged links during the eighteenth century with a number of notables across the Atlantic. With the outbreak of hostilities between Britain and the American colonies in the 1770s, a small group of loyalist refugees from New England chose to settle in the town. Samuel Curwen, a judge of the Admiralty Court of Massachusetts, lodged with one of the Folletts at the Mill House and kept a diary of his stay there; the Rev. Isaac Smith actually became minister of the Old Meeting; and a third refugee, Governor Hutchinson of Massachusetts was the great-grandfather of Sidmouth's celebrated eccentric nineteenth-century historian Peter Orlando Hutchinson.

The fishing industry was not the only Sidmouth institution struggling in the eighteenth century. The Prideaux family was in difficulty. The financial embarrassment started in 1729 when the lord of the manor, Edmund Prideaux, died leaving £2,000 each to his daughters. The next baronet, John, did not pay that sum nor the interest on it and the debt increased with startling rapidity. By 1778 we find the manor in Chancery where it was decreed that the manor was to be sold if the debts could not be paid. Oliver Cromwell, attorney acting for Thomas Jenkins, bid the sum of £15,600.

Thomas Jenkins, born in 1722 in Honiton, made his fortune in Rome where he first cleaned and restored pictures and dabbled in various kinds of antiques, but then proceeded to manufacture sham antiques which were palmed off as genuine. He subsequently set up in business as a banker, patronized by English visitors and residents. In 1773, he had purchased Bindon near Axmouth, and also Cotford in Sidbury. In 1797 he drew up a will in bad Italian which, both in that language and when translated into English, gave rise to many disputes and several lawsuits among his numerous descendants. The will reveals the anxiety felt for securing the estates for ever in the male line and the pride which he felt at the prospect of becoming the founder of a family. In the spring of 1798 he wound up his affairs in Rome and proceeded to return to England but he was taken ill on board ship and having landed at Great Yarmouth, he died there on 11th May, without ever seeing his treasured purchase. In due course his great-nephew, Thomas, a captain of Dragoons, took possession of the manor of Sidmouth.

Exmouth and Teignmouth had been attracting West-country gentry and Exeter merchants since the 1750s, when medical opinion decided that sea-water had the same beneficial properties as spa water. Isaac Curwen, in his diary for 1776, remarks that in Sidmouth there was much "genteel company resorting to the town for the benefit of sea-bathing" but it was in the 1790s that Sidmouth's mild climate, scenic beauties and relatively cheap accommodation became more widely known among the nobility and gentry, especially of Bath and Bristol. The wars on the Continent had put a stop to wintering abroad. In 1801, Jane Austen is thought to have spent a family summer holiday in Sidmouth where she fell in love with the brother of a local doctor, but he was called away on business and died of typhus in Bath. In the churchyard, there is a sad monument to Mary Lisle from Northumberland who died in February 1791 at the age of 39:

"Blest with soft airs from health restoring skies,
Sidmouth! to thee the drooping patient flies:
Ah! not unfailing is thy port to save,
To her thou gavist no refuge, but a grave:
Guard it, mild Sidmouth, and revere its store,
More precious, none shall ever touch thy shore."

Dunscombe Cliffs
by H. Haseler and D. Havell pubd. by J. Wallis

The Devon coast was becoming a retirement area for invalids, particularly returned East India Company officials but, in 1801, at the first census return, Sidmouth, remote from London and from most of the other fashionable centres, was still a small resort with a population of 1,252. Yet the boom had begun and once more it was the sea that proved the principal source of prosperity for Sidmouth.

THE REGENCY PERIOD
I – BACKGROUND

Sidmouth is often referred to as a 'Regency town'; it was during this brief period that the town became a fashionable resort. Because of the importance of the period, a general description of the town at this time will be followed by a closer look at the period's unique and much admired architecture. George IV (1820-30) was regent only from 1811 to 1820, but, as the ferment of new ideas and styles began before that, we will copy most people in choosing as 'Regency' 1795 to 1830.

Thomas Jenkins, the Lord of the Manor, died in 1798 without seeing his property. He left it to his great-nephew, also Thomas Jenkins, a captain of Dragoons, who saw the Manor map that William Day had made in 1789 and realised that earlier Lords of the Manor had given him a marvellously untouched and cosy little valley with a relaxed air.

Peak House – drawn from Nature on stone by G. Rowe, printed by P. Simonau and pubd. by J. Wallis 1826

The town nestled neatly in the angle between river and sea, with an astonishing extent of the old strip-fields. The western half of the valley was almost devoid of houses with one exception. In 1793, Emanuel Baruch Lousada, a rich and cultured Jew, had bought initially 75 acres, including Peeke Tenement, and added a further 50 acres shortly afterwards. He purchased the land from Sir William Pole, the owner of Old Hayes (now Woodlands). A Jew's right of entitlement to

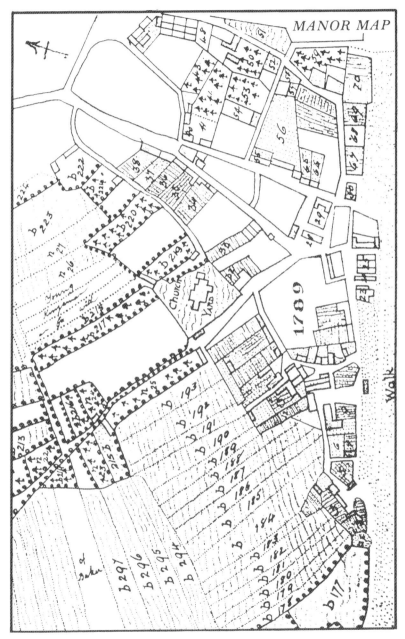

Manor Map by William Day, 1789

property was uncertain and "only the most courageous dared to buy". He joined at once into Sidmouth life and responsibilities and by buying up most of Peak Hill and much else he became the second-largest landowner in the valley. Peak House stands out alone on the hillside in the first published picture of Sidmouth drawn by the elder Rowe in 1796. Lousada and his nephew of the same name were given the same glowing dedication in each state of the Long Picture in 1815 and 1840. (The original of this picture may be seen in the Museum). They set up relatives in Belmont and Rosemount and bought other houses.

Sidmouth from Salcombe Hill 1796 – first known engraving of Sidmouth, original by G. Rowe, Senr. engraved and pubd. by G. Walker

It is often said that people came to Devon because Napoleon had put a stop to the Grand Tour, but they were few compared with the numbers who had caught the rage for "tours to portray the native elegance of their own clime". Devon attracts such folk with its beauty and warmth and the rustic charm of the talk and the cottages of cob and thatch, "grown out of the earth" said Cosimo III, Grand Duke of Tuscany.

"This was the heyday of English watercolourists with more first-class artists than before or since". The invention of aquatint in 1773 and of the lithograph in 1808 enabled the works of these men to be reproduced cheaply and they became extremely popular. The guiding spirit of this movement was Ackermann of 101, Strand. A close associate of his was John Wallis who published a great variety of games and puzzles and sent his son John to Sidmouth to cater for the booming market of topography. Young John started well at the original library

Wallis Marine Library – now the site of the Bedford Hotel, pubd. by J. Wallis 1817

by Beach House but, in 1809, moved to the site of the Bedford Hotel, also called the Shed or, later, the Lounge. Wallis's Marine Library with billiards and a shop was thus in a central position on the Beach. Sidmouth owes its Museum collection of over 250 pictures of houses and coastal views largely to this enterprising man who also published Hubert Cornish's Long Picture of the sea-front in 1815. A result of all this artistic activity was that Sidmouth grew rapidly. New houses were built and others enlarged. The fashion of the day was Regency Gothic.

There were several reasons why people came to Sidmouth in particular and often to build here. One was the cliffs that enclose the Front so nobly and the "lofty mountains" (Butcher!) around the valley with their exciting or terrifying gradients on Old Peak, Old Trow and Salcombe Hills and, worst of all, the Pinn hairpins on the old Honiton "main" road, by no means free from danger to a coach, and needing oxen. They gave an exclusive, almost secret, feel to the valley. Such circumstances would appeal to seasoned Continental travellers. The word got around London and the names of people who had settled here helped a lot. Lord le Despencer let his house at Knowle to the Marquess of Bute; the Duke and Duchess of Kent with their baby Victoria lived at Woolbrook Cottage for a short time; and Lord Gwydir at Woodlands was such a close friend of the Regent

View of Sidmouth descending Salcombe Hill 1819
by E.I J. Esq., R. Ackermann's Lithographic Press, pubd. by J. Wallis 1819

himself that the newspapers reported on the Coronation that at 10.25 a.m. on 19th July, 1821 the King entered Westminster Hall and was 25 minutes late because "his Lord Great Chamberlain, Lord Gwydir, had torn his clothes while trying to get into them."

The first writer about local affairs was the Rev. Edmund Butcher who had come to the area from London to recover from a chest infection and was a minister of the Unitarian chapel. He left Helens, the house given to him by Lousada, on an excursion to Chester in 1803. He wrote regular letters in a fulsome fruity style. Astonishingly he had only reached Sidbury when he devoted two pages of vituperation to the "multitude" of small children "who here become sallow and languid working a ten-hour day in making lace, sacrificing health to unnecessary articles of female decoration". On his return, the social walk known as the Beach "had been beautifully rolled and there was more building in the town, particularly on the slopes". Most houses of all sizes were taking lodgers. The Assembly Rooms were at the London Inn in Fore Street and in need of a Master of Ceremonies for introductions and advice. Was one ever appointed, we wonder?

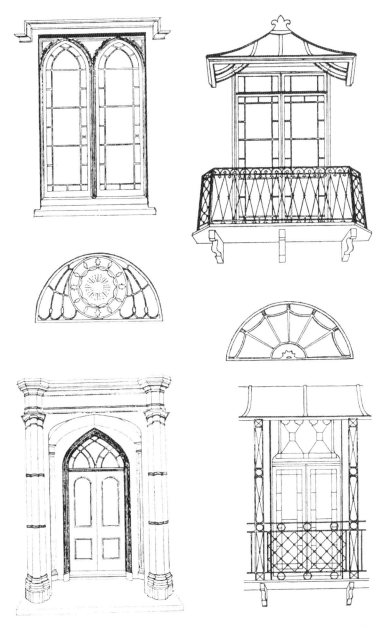

*Regency Features in Sidmouth – from the smaller Queen Anne and Georgian House
by Harry Forrester, Tindal Press. Reprinted by permission of J. H. Clarke & Co., Ltd*

COTTAGE ORNÉ

drawn from Nature on stone by G. Rowe, printed by P. Simonau pubd. by J. Wallis 1826

Knowle Cottage, Sidmouth

Woodbine Cottage

STRAWBERRY HILL GOTHIC

Coburg Terrace, Sidmouth
drawn from Nature on stone by G. Rowe, printed by P. Simonau pubd. by J. Wallis 1826

Belmont House pubd. by J. Wallis 1817

THE REGENCY PERIOD II – HOUSES

Illustrations in this chapter were drawn from nature on stone by G. Rowe, printed by P. Simonau pubd. by J. Wallis 1826, unless otherwise stated.

The architects responsible for the simple, well-proportioned houses of the Georgian period began to be influenced in the late 18th century by a revival of interest in the Gothic style and a more relaxed and even frivolous mood. The discovery that iron could be cast into fine decorative shapes encouraged the production of stock patterns for general use in balconies and balustrades, and stained glass became more widely available. These new trends found eloquent expression in the houses built for the nobility and gentry who were attracted to Sidmouth. The population grew from 1,252 in 1801 to 3,441 by 1851.

Fortfield Terrace – Visit of Grand Duchess Hélène in 1831
by G. Rowe, printed by Engelmann & Co., pubd. by J. Harvey.

Similar developments in Bath and Brighton produced fine terraces, and the year 1792 saw the building of the brick-faced Fortfield Terrace by a young Polish architect, Novoselski, trained in Italy. No. 8 with its triangular pediment was intended to be the centre and the design was planned to extend westward, but his early death prevented its completion; otherwise our much-valued cricket field with its pavilion in use since the 1820s would not have played its part in Sidmouth life. The first-floor balconies and tent-shaped canopies were added later. Princess Caroline of Brunswick, the estranged wife of the Prince Regent, stayed briefly in 1806 as the guest of Lord Gwydir. Grand Duchess Helena Pavlovna, sister in law of the Russian Tsar stayed in 1831; hence the Russian Eagle mounted in the pediment of numbers 7 and 8.

The distinguished "incomers" who quickly followed were able to indulge their individual fancies for a rural retreat in an ornamented and thatched cottage style known as the 'cottage orné' or in the mode made popular by Horace Walpole in his 'Strawberry Hill Gothic' villa at Twickenham, with its castellated battlements and elaborate Gothicised windows and embellishments. Sidmouth is unique in showing both these Regency developments to their maximum advantage in individual forms.

Walking around the town one sees elegant iron balconies with tent-shaped or pointed canopies, and carved iron or wooden supports in Gothic designs and trellis patterns. The colonial administrators and military men who retired here were accustomed to wide verandahs and sweeping lawns, and the general use of white stucco and silver-grey tiled roofs gave an effect of light which our more than averagely sunny climate enhanced. Windows have infinite variety, from the simple Georgian wooden-sashed type with narrow but strong glazing bars to pointed patterned ones often incorporating stained glass. Painted drip moulds above are a noticeable feature. Roofs are edged with carved boards of many designs such as scallops and trefoils. Porches often have carved and ornamented pillar or trellis supports and doorways are surmounted with delicately traced fanlights.

Woodlands in Station Road, a fantastic example of Regency work with later added ornamentation, was originally a mediaeval farmhouse called "Old Hayes", and was converted in 1806 by Lord Gwydir to a cottage orné. The thatch was replaced in 1850 with pleasing hexagonal tiles and ornate ridge tiles, edged on the gables with very elaborate pink barge boards made from Italian terracotta. Opposite is Powys built in 1820 by Miss Wright as a long one-storeyed thatched cottage orné, later enlarged and tiled and recently expanded still further with a block of flats! On the opposite corner is Audley, once the home of the Dowager Lady Audley, converted in

1830 from a cottage orné into a gracious Georgian-style building with a pillared portico; now the centre for a pleasing matching modern development of houses. Nearby in All Saints Road is Cedar Shade which, converted from a farmhouse, exemplifies the Colonial ideal and has immense charm, with wide eaves and cedar-shaded lawns. Ornate French windows lead to trellised verandahs and there is also an octagonal Regency conservatory.

Further up Station Road is Claremont, erected in 1825 but burnt down and restored in 1845 with handsome balconies. Here lived Louisa and Charlotte, daughters of the Earl of Buckinghamshire. Opposite is Knowle, now a large unattractive building but with a fascinating history. It was built between 1805 and 1809 by Lord le Despencer. It was then a very large and charming thatched cottage orné with 40 rooms, and was bought in 1821 by Mr Fish, a wealthy man who filled the house with objets d'art and the garden with rare trees and shrubs, fountains, statues, and exotic birds and animals, all of which people came many miles to see. It was open on Mondays only in August and September. Children and dogs were banned and it closed if it was raining. Between 1867 and 1882 the owner was Richard Thornton, a respected local philanthropist, who made many radical changes. In 1882 it was converted into an hotel, with further alterations to entirely obscure the cottage orné appearance of 60 years before. It was further expanded into the East Devon District Council Offices, and the original house became unrecognisable.

In lower Station Road, twin thatched cottages of early date, Gwydir and Larbi Cote, form a charming vista framing the tree-lined road to Knowle. The house, Milestones, has iron flower-guards to the upper windows and shows the flint walls and gateway piers so characteristic of Sidmouth. A little further down, in Coburg Road, is Alma Terrace built of red brick in the post-Regency period to commemorate the battle of the Alma in 1854. It has many Regency features, beautiful windows and unusual ornamental porches with peaked canopies.

Nearby is Kennaway House, originally called Fort House, in a dominating position, built in red brick about 1812, with wide curved steps and balustrade, pillared porch, and a door with a notable fanlight. 'Aurora', at the side, has delicate balconies and a door

Lodge to the Marino

Richmond House, now Sidholme

Powys Cotttage

Camden Cottage, Elysian Fields

Clifton Cottage

Woodlands – now Woodlands Hotel, from the garden,

Cotmaton House

Woodlands Front

Myrtle Cottage

Sid Abbey

Woolbrook Cottage, now Royal Glen
by H. Haseler & D. Havell, pubd. by J. Wallis 1819

Fort House, now Kennaway House
by H. Haseler & D. Havell, pubd. by J. Wallis 1816

Fort House facing west

Amyat Place, now Amyatts Terrace
also showing Hope Cottage, Sidmouth Museum, pubd. by J. Wallis 1817

leading to a hall with an elegant curved staircase and an iron balustrade, a beautiful example of Regency design. Behind is Barton Cottage, once the home of Miss Cash, who embroidered names and monograms on linen which became 'Cash's Name Tapes'.

Coburg Terrace overlooking the Bowling Green was built between 1820 and 1825 in Strawberry Hill Gothic style. It consists of four houses with a castellated parapet, Gothicised windows, and a fine porch with balconies to the first floor windows.

Woolbrook Cottage – from the garden

An even finer example of Strawberry Hill Gothic is the Royal Glen converted from the earlier Woolbrook Cottage. This has a castellated parapet, striking Gothicised windows and drip moulds, a beautiful verandah and handsome porch. Modern extensions are in harmony. Here the Duke of Kent in December 1819, embarrassed by creditors and liking our climate, brought the Duchess and his baby, later Queen Victoria, to stay. A local boy catapulted a stone which narrowly missed the little Princess. The Duke's love for his daughter, whom he called "My little May Blossom", is well-known. At his Christmas dinner he seated her on a cushion in the centre, saying, "She is the sweetest dish on the table". His devotion probably led to his death, for instead of changing his clothes after a wet walk, he insisted on playing with the baby and later developed a fatal fever.

West view of Sidmouth from the beach also showing Chit Rock,
by H. Haseler printed by C. Hullmandel, pubd. by Haseler 1825

The west end of the Esplanade is occupied by one of Sidmouth's most characteristic features – Clifton Place – originally Heffer's Row. The Heffer family, although fishermen, built first one and then another as lodging houses (nos 4 and 5). Nos 2 and 3 were two cottages and Rock Cottage was a lodging house. Clifton Cottage had been a picnic house for the Lousadas from Peak House and was converted to a dwelling, lived in by Haseler, the drawing master. The Beacon was not built until 1842. Beacon, Rock and Clifton Cottages are all re-builds following fire damage. Below this on the beach were a few cottages where 'Dame Partington' is supposed to have tried to repel the ocean with her broom. The story was related by its inventor, the writer Sidney Smith, as an example of the futility of the House of Lords trying to stop the reform of Parliament. These cottages together with Chit Rock were swept away by the great storm of 1824.

The Esplanade itself has a picturesque collection of hotels with interesting histories. Belmont, a family house, was enlarged in 1820 and has since been much extended as an hotel. It originally had a long castellated front wall and gateway but now only the gateway remains. The Riviera, with its echoes of the South of France, was a terrace of three-storey lodging houses and is recognisable as Marine Place in the 1814 Long Picture. The Bedford Hotel is bound up with the town's early history. John Wallis's Marine Library was transferred here in 1809, and one can imagine, in its verandah, the meeting of the fashionable under the patronage of Lord and Lady Despencer, Lord Gwydir, Lady Willoughby and Emanuel Lousada, to read the news and indulge in the latest gossip. Afterwards they would transfer to the Assembly Rooms at the London Inn, later named the Royal London Hotel (now converted into shops and flats), to dance upstairs on its sprung floor or to play cards.

Beach House, the York Hotel & Marsh's Library
pubd. by J Wallis 1820

Beach House is a Regency jewel. Its pillared and vaulted porch, Gothicised stained glass windows with drip moulds over, delicate ironwork to balconies on carved brackets, tent-shaped canopies and scalloped eaves boards are an evocation of the atmosphere of that time and Sidmouth's heritage. A number of houses show many varieties of Regency design: their verandahs and balconies, canopies with carved pillar supports and graceful fanlights over doors add interest to the pleasure of a seaside holiday.

Marino Lodge in Cotmaton Road must be the most unusual ex-Council house in Britain. It was the lodge of Pauntley, originally the Marino in the early 19th century, which became later the home of W. H. Smith, Viscount Hambledon, who gave the cottage to the town on condition that his chauffeur's family, who had lived there for fifty years, could continue to do so for their lifetime. It has pointed windows and a domed thatched roof carried out to form a verandah supported by posts with linking archway. Nearby are the White Cottage, Cotmaton House and some delightful houses with Regency style features, old and modern! Eaglehurst in Seafield Road has a lovely carved doorway almost hidden underground, and further down the road are Littlecourt with extravagant curved balconies, Seacourt and Seafield with attractive windows and elaborately carved eaves boards and gables, Eglantine with trellised balconies, and Pebblestone Cottage which lives up to its name.

Violet Bank Cottage, now Littlecourt
pubd. by J. Wallis 1820

From Radway, north past the building which had been the Main Post Office, along Vicarage Road, the Hermitage, Balsters and The Shrubbery are worthy of note and lead to Elysian Fields, a planned development in 1826 of typical Regency-style villas set in large grounds. Sidholme, now a Christian Guild Holiday Hotel, then owned by the 6th Earl of Buckinghamshire, has a magnificent pillared music room in Classical style with an organ and chandeliers hanging from a painted ceiling, built when the Countess quarrelled with the vicar and decided to have services there. It is now a lovely setting for some of Sidmouth's musical events.

Salcombe House, now Hunter's Moon Hotel

Spanning the River Sid is the Stone Bridge (or Waterloo Bridge) and beyond it the Doric-pillared Toll House. In Sid Road are some houses of special note: Salcombe House (1770), now Hunter's Moon Hotel; Salcombe Lodge (1810) with a perfect Regency facade; and further along Sid Abbey in Fortescue. Sid Abbey was converted early in the 19th century from the stables of Sidcliffe Farm; it was never an abbey but built in the best romantic traditions with steep battlemented gables.

The Duchess of Kent with Princess Victoria
by Sir William Beechey is reproduced by Gracious permission of Her Majesty the Queen

THE VICTORIAN AGE

When the 18-year old Princess Victoria became queen in 1837 she was no stranger here. In infancy she stayed with her parents the Duke and Duchess of Kent at Woolbrook Cottage (now the Royal Glen Hotel) in 1819. The visit was brief as the Duke died suddenly in January 1820. The cortège left for Windsor with black-draped mourners, carriages and horses. It was a long-remembered royal occasion. The event is recorded on a plaque on the east wall of the hotel.

Sidmouth had become a favoured watering place. Risdon's "one of the especialest fisher towns of the shire" in the early 17th century had developed into a prosperous small town; the newcomers had sought homes and health cures in the sheltered valleys of the south coast. Among the new residents were retired service, professional and clerical families with some titled people. Ample domestic help was available at the prevailing low wages. With servants, grooms and gardeners to attend them, life was comfortable and easy for the incomers. New houses had been built and estates made on farmland away from the town.

Travellers often preferred the sea routes to journeys by coach. Landing over the shingle banks was hazardous and at times impossible. In spite of the difficulties, boats were built in a yard on the site of York Terrace as late as the 1860s; they were launched over the shingle and taken to Exmouth for rigging. The increasing coastal trade caused demands for a harbour. Coal and heavy goods came by sea, special lime for the kilns on the west cliff came from Torbay and was landed on western beach. The first of several harbour projects was proposed in 1811. Architects, engineers and solicitors were employed and detailed plans prepared. In each case, the funds failed before any harbour appeared. The third harbour project in 1834 was an ambitious one. It was to be at the west end of the front and suitable stone was to be brought on a light railway from Hook Ebb, to the east of the river mouth. A tunnel was made through the red cliff by the river and a steam engine was purchased and brought by sea; alas and alack, the engine was found to be too large for the tunnel! There was a joyride along the rails before engine and project vanished from recorded history. In the same year (1834), at the suggestion of John Wallis, the Esplanade was constructed. It

Sidmouth's intended harbour
printed by J. Graf, pubd. by J. Harvey

improved conditions on the sea-front as well as giving some protection from the occasional floods and storms.

Sidmouth owes its collections of 252 prints of houses and coastal views largely to Wallis, who also published Hubert Cornish's Long Picture of the Front with Wallis's Marine library, billiard-room and shop in the centre with a fashionable throng.

Roads were still maintained by the Turnpike authorities, and toll houses are mentioned in the records. Sidmouth has a survivor built about 1817 – the little dwelling just east of Salcombe (Waterloo) Bridge. In 1985, the tollgate was mended and rehung as part of the new entrance to the Byes built by the Sid Vale Association.

Carriage entrance to Knowle Cottage
by T. Fidlor & T. Sutherland, pubd. by J. Wallis 1823

All Saints' Church, Sidmouth
from notepaper by J.S. & Co. c. 1855

The Town Mill, on the western bank of the Ford, dates also from 1817. The wheel was powered from a leet which arose just above the man-made waterfall of the River Sid in the first field of the Byes and ran parallel to the river. It remained a working mill until early in the 20th century.

The Tithe Apportionment Survey of 1841 gives a complete picture of the parish. Each holding with its owner and occupier is named, each field is named and its acreage and use given, with the tithe assessment. In 1851, the Ordnance Survey map-makers came to the district, causing great interest. "Spot the O.S. marks" became a new game on outings. In the same year, the common land was enclosed on Salcombe hilltop, with the loss of the racecourse as well as common pasture.

All Saints' Church was built in 1837 on land given by Sir John Kennaway of Escot who owned property in Sidmouth bought from the Manor Estate. The area between Sidmouth and Sidbury having become more populous, a church was desired at Sidford. St. Peter's was built and divine service was held for the first time on 3 September 1868. The Unitarian and Congregational chapels had been established in the 18th century; the Methodist chapel was built in Victorian times.

Education prior to the 20th century was usually associated with churches (often referred to as parochial schools – belonging to the parish). There are references to Trust Deeds for the Sidmouth Parochial Boys' School in 1663, 1744 and 1827. Until 1922 when the co-educational Senior School was built off Vicarage Road, now the infants section of Sidmouth Primary School, it was housed in a building in Mill Street which is now converted to Counter's Court. The two entrances still bear the faded names of "Girls" and "Boys". The pretty schoolmaster's cottage still adjoins it. Not far away, nearer the sea, in a schoolroom now demolished, was the Parochial Girls' and Infants' School founded in 1858 though one existed previously. There was also a Church School at Woolbrook established in 1878 but in 1907 it was in such a bad state of repair that it was replaced by a new Council School.

Many Church of England Schools applied for union with the National Society for Promoting Religious Education which laid down conditions about teaching and staff. All Saints, which sought membership in 1848, was such a school. A year or two before, an enquiry into Church Schools showed that it then had 51 boys and 102 girls. A Dame School with 3 boys and 17 girls is also recorded. The two parochial schools catered for 77 boys, 70 girls and 20 infants.

Sidbury also had a National School which began in 1830 as a Sunday School and developed into a Day School. The Society gave £175 towards the estimated cost of £250 for building and fitting the school. Local gentry contributed another £40 towards the venture while farmers lent horses and carts to draw the materials. The estimated annual charge for teacher and books was £131. However, by 1848 when the daily attendance was 57, (the Sunday School numbers ranged from 100 to 150), the mistress received £38 per annum, books cost £3 and items like fuel and candles £1.7s.6d. Fees from the children's parents brought in £8 to £9. An Infants' School existed at Sidford from 1860 to 1923 and a deed of 1907 says it belonged to Sir Charles Cave, Lord of the Manor of Sidbury, who let it on annual rent of one shilling. Salcombe Regis Sunday and Charity School, founded in 1820, came under the aegis of the National Society in 1833. It began in a building adjacent to the Church which had been the Poor House; the Cornishes then built a purpose-designed little thatched school on the hill overlooking the Church.

Sidmouth remained a mainly self-supporting community. Meat, game, poultry, dairy produce and fish were all local products. Produce, including early potatoes were grown on sheltered 'plats' on the cliff side of Branscombe, using seaweed as a fertiliser. Donkeys carried the vegetables and fruit up the steep path to the top. This tradition continued into the mid 20th century. Vegetables and fruit were supplied by market gardens and from the well-stocked gardens and glasshouses of the gentry. Every farm had an apple orchard and made its own cider. Sea-fishing was a major occupation and huge catches were recorded, mainly of mackerel, herring and sprats. The River Sid provided salmon peal, trout, crayfish and lampreys. (Alma footbridge at its mouth, like Alma Terrace, is a reminder of the Crimean War of 1854-6).

Sea-bathing had long been popular partly for health reasons and in Victorian times bathers were drawn down to the water's edge in modest little machines. Sidmouth had a lifeboat in 1869, presented

Ghosts, sketch by Peter Orlando Hutchinson
reprinted by permission of the Devon Record Office

by Mrs. Rimington. With its twelve-man crew it was paraded through the town before being launched. It then capsized! Later it did good work along the coast, for wrecks and bathing accidents were frequent. The Rev. Richard Kirwan, rector of Gittisham, was drowned bathing alone. He was an ardent treasure-seeking despoiler of Bronze Age burial mounds on the hills. P.O.H. was critical of such excavating; he had quite a modern attitude and was a pioneer of scientific research.

The new age was one of scientific discovery in many directions. There was an effervescent reaction to the exciting future prospects. Sidmouth shared in the stimulating search for knowledge. Some of the well-educated and leisured men such as the Rev. N. S. Heineken were active in their studies and produced work of real value. Some of the earliest lithographs were drawn and processed in Sidmouth, and musical instruments and telescopes were made and used by these enterprising gentlemen.

*19th Century Honiton
lace from Sidmouth
Museum's collection*

*Bobbin lace collar
and cuff made by
Dame Harriette Chick*

Lace motifs

*Each lace-maker
specialised in a
particular motif
and the various
designs were then
combined to make
collars, mats, etc.*

Peter Orlando Hutchinson

Fire was a constant hazard. The old Radway mill was destroyed in a blaze in which one man died. On other occasions houses, shops, farm buildings and town stables were burnt out.

Pillow lace-making was a flourishing local craft centred on Honiton and the whole East Devon area, including Sidmouth. The cushion and bobbins needed for the delicate work were seen in many cottages. There were several shops and agents in the town. Mrs Hayman and Mrs Mitchell had a lace shop, Banwell House, in Old Fore Street from the 1840s. Subsequently, the Barnard family

Belle Vue, now Cedar Shade
drawn from Nature on stone by G. Rowe, printed by P. Simonau, pubd. by J. Wallis 1826

continued in the same premises until the 1960s. Miss Barnard proudly displayed on a board the Royal Arms granted by the Duchess of Kent. This treasure is now in the Museum together with a fine selection of Victorian lace. Miss Barnard's great-grandmother, Mrs. Nicholls, had made lace for Princess Victoria and the Duchess of Kent in 1830 and her grandmother, Mrs. Hayman, made the wedding lace for Princess Christian. Queen Adelaide and Princess Beatrice were also customers. Lace-making declined towards the end of the century, but there has been a welcome revival in modern times.

Two well-known writers have associations with Sidmouth. The father of Elizabeth Barrett (Browning) had lost heavily on his Jamaican plantations through the abolition of the slavery trade. He sold the family mansion, Hope End, in Herefordshire. He came to Sidmouth in 1832 and rented 6-8 Fortfield Terrace where the family stayed for 12 months. Elizabeth at that time was very withdrawn, but enjoyed the ocean views though she found the town rather dull with its "cricket and croquet". In 1833 the family moved to Cedar Shade, then called Belle Vue. Elizabeth, mounted on a donkey, accompanied her brothers on their routine walks along lanes, up Salombe Hill and on the edge of the sea. Elizabeth formed her first romantic attachment with the minister of the Congregational Chapel, George Hunter. They were in love but the affair gradually faded, although they remained friends until his death in 1857. The family left for Wimpole Street in 1835.

William Makepeace Thackeray (1811-63) knew the district well. He spent some months between leaving Charterhouse and going to Trinity College, Cambridge, on his step-father's estate at Larkbeare near Talaton. He enjoyed the social life and wrote about it in 'The History of Pendennis', a largely autobiographical book published in 1849/50. Places and people are thinly disguised. Thus Ottery St. Mary becomes Clavering St Mary, while Sidmouth is Baymouth. Class distinctions were still well-marked with the landed gentry having a supercilious attitude toward everybody else. In an account of a ball at The London Hotel at Sidmouth, Thackeray describes the costumes – the tight-fitting red jackets of the Dragoon Guards for instance, and the fantastic hair styles of the ladies.

Societies sprang up to support and advance their own interests. The Sid Vale Association founded in 1846, was the first amenity society in England. The Devonshire Association came into being in 1862 and a Sidmouth branch was formed after World War Two. These societies are still very active. A sense of civic duty and responsibility had developed with the increasing wealth of the town. There had been many benefactors in the past who had left property, goods and money to sustain the destitute and needy. Sidmouth had the Poor Lands administered by the Feoffees, the Poor House for the homeless, and the church charities. The new objective, as in all Britain, was towards improving the quality of life. Many clubs and societies were founded to cater for every interest. One of the first was a cricket club, formed in 1823: balls had long been kicked about on the Fort Field, but this was the beginning of organised sport. An archery club was formed in 1858 which practised in the grounds of Cotmaton and Peak Houses. Croquet also started in 1858 – imported from France, it became all the rage. Tennis began towards the end of the century, on private courts, with tournaments organised in places like Torquay.

There was a Needlework Society for the ladies. In a man's world the wives and daughters had to be content with restricted lives; much of their time was occupied with paying and receiving calls, attending parties and balls, and making expeditions on foot or by carriage with any gentleman able to escort them. The carriages had delightful names: fly, gig, phaeton (with one or two horses), chaise or bath chair among them. There was a daily coach to Exeter via Ottery St. Mary and the carrier was in demand for the transport of heavy goods. A reminder of past grandeur was recorded when Lady Rolle of Bicton was seen in her coach and four, with outriders, driving on Woodbury Common in 1864. There were several stables in Sidmouth from which

New Fort, sketch by Peter Orlando Hutchinson,
reprinted by permission of the Devon Record Office

horses and carriages could be hired. Tricycles and bicycles made their appearance in 1868 causing astonished disapproval as well as excited interest. There was, however, an escort of tricycles for a Devonshire Association carriage outing, which probably produced as much amazement as it might today. After a nasty cycle accident on Trow Hill enthusiasm dwindled in the hilly district.

The ladies were excited when the crinoline became the fashion. There is an account of a Christmas Ball in 1862, held in the London Hotel Assembly Rooms – a shambles of torn material, flounces and ribbons was left on the floor after the congestion caused by the ladies' enormous hooped dresses. Collecting was another occupation for young ladies, guided and instructed by any gentleman so inclined. The collections included pebbles, usually polished, geological specimens, fossils, shells, curiosities, coins, engravings, wild flowers, ferns and seaweed. Sketching and drawing were a part of all good education: before the days of the camera, sketch books provided a record of visits and travel. P.O.H. was especially gifted: he had taken lessons, with his lifelong friend C. F. Williams, from a German artist. Williams was the son of a harpist in the service of the Courtenays of Powderham Castle before retiring to Sidmouth. He became a well-known painter and lithographer.

The Volunteer Artillery and Rifle Corps were formed in 1859 as a result of strained relations with the Emperor Napoleon III and kept some of the retired service men usefully occupied. The troops included men of all groups: they drilled on the Fort Field, paraded through the town, and exercised on Peak and Salcombe hills, as well as competing with other troops further afield. Two twenty-four pound guns were obtained, which added a new dimension to the many celebrations held. Gun salutes, bands and flags honoured Royal weddings and birthdays, the end of the Russian war, Waterloo Day, and other special occasions. P.O.H. was an enthusiast with his guns in the partially rebuilt Sidmouth Fort. The Volunteer Artillery was disbanded in 1871. Troops of yeomanry and cavalry were quartered in Sidmouth for a week's summer manoeuvres during the 1860s. These military visitors were quite a thrill for the young ladies. Parties and dances were arranged, and the spectacle of reviews and drills added to the events of the season, with a fine show of red coats for Sunday Church parades.

Public Service increased as various Boards came about. The Local Government Board, the Railway and Hospital Boards and the Burial Board (formed when the churchyard was closed and the cemetery constructed), all provided useful work and interest. The first scheme for a branch railway line was mooted in 1856, when the Southern line was advancing towards Honiton and Exeter. Sufficient

Sidmouth Parish Church
by H. Haseler, printed by C. Hullmandel, pubd. by Haseler 1825

funds could not be raised and it was not until the seventies that a second project was successful. It was sponsored by the Trustees of the Manor Estate: the proposed route was via Bowd, through Harpford Woods to Tipton St. John and Ottery St. Mary. Capital of £66,000 was authorised, a site for the station chosen and contracts signed. Visits to watch progress were frequent and anticipation intense. On 9th July, 1874 the line was opened amid scenes of jubilation and pride. Sidmouth was "almost beside itself" was one eye-witness's report. Parties were given for everyone in the town; the shareholders were wined and dined. It is hard to believe that this delightful line has gone, destroyed by the Beeching economies – with

First Old Chancel of Sidmouth Parish Church, 1859
sketch by Peter Orlando Hutchinson reprinted by permission of the Devon Record Office

The Old Chancel 1880
sketch by Peter Orlando Hutchinson reprinted by permission of the Devon Record Office

much of the track returned to farm use, or converted into footpaths and cycle ways.

By the mid-century, Sidmouth had become a wealthy community and, in 1858, it was decided to improve the parish church. This restoration was an almost complete rebuilding, except for the tower and the nave arcades. The vicar, the Rev. H. Hamilton, the curate, the Rev. G. Deacon, two churchwardens (Messrs. Webber and Prettijohn), Mr. B. Lousada, J.P. (nephew of the original builder of Peak House), and P.O.H. were elected at a public meeting to supervise the project. But P.O.H. soon found himself at variance with the others. They wanted a fine new building whereas he wished to preserve the best of the old one. Shocked at the wholesale destruction of the chancel and the mediaeval glass, he arranged with the contractor to move the chancel stones and east window to his land beside his home at 4, Coburg Terrace and there built a smaller version, at a cost of £45. A second room was added by the purchase of stones and a window from Awliscombe Church for £4 as that was also being "restored". He embellished the interior of the 'Old Chancel', as it is still called, with many examples of his interests: beautiful panelling and ceilings, stained glass and carved mantelpieces and doors. Within the church itself P.O.H. managed to get some pieces of carved stone reset high up in the walls, two incised slabs and, most important, a small window of mediaeval glass showing the five wounds of Christ placed in the vestry which is now the Lady Chapel.

Opinions in the town became inflamed as the Low Church No-Popery faction accused the architect and Committee of High Church objectives under the influence of the Oxford or Tractarian movement. Posters, preserved in the Museum, show the depth of feeling aroused. The grand re-opening of the church, in July 1860 did not end the disagreements about the restoration, for a furious row blew up over the placement of the Queen's window at the west end as it meant the removal of the newly installed organ to the east end near the altar. Backed by the Earl of Buckinghamshire, P.O.H. decided upon drastic action. He went by coach to Honiton and by the new train to Cowes, changed into his dress uniform of the Volunteer Artillery with sword and walked to Osborne House. He did not see Queen Victoria herself but was allowed to leave a petition with a covering letter explaining the position. On his return he was deeply hurt to be insulted in newspapers and letters. However, tempers cooled and, after the vicar and curate had left Sidmouth, the window given by the Queen in memory of her father the Duke of Kent was placed in the west end of the church.

New arrivals in the town created the need for new buildings of all kinds: Fields and Potburys are examples of good Victorian building, and the names of these firms' owners appeared on local Boards and Committees for several generations. In the main shopping area, the shops are mainly conversions of old houses as can be seen by looking at the upper floors and windows. Potburys in the High Street (1849), now as then a furniture shop, has a heavy carved doorway and windows which have the slender colonettes which break up an unattractive expanse of glass, and are characteristic of older shop windows in the town. Opposite is a shop which until recently, belonged to a long established butchers, Holmes. Its striking front, with the original projecting counter behind, had a brass name-plate with brass column supports to a heavy cornice and blind-case and the upper part of the door was still slatted for ventilation. Trumps, established in 1813, was a high-class grocery and provision shop and has a pleasing mid-19th century frontage; inside are some of the original mahogany counters, shelves and fittings. On the western side of Market Place in 1810 were two adjacent properties, both occupied by drapers. Later in the century, John Field, also a draper, bought these properties and developed Sidmouth's first department store.

The red-brick Manor House (now flats) was built on the site of Broadway farm and house by the Trustees of the estate, appointed by George Edmund Balfour of Manchester, who bought it in 1868 at a reputed cost of £82,000. He lived at Powys for a few years, but died leaving three orphan children, his wife having predeceased him. Sidmouth had at last got a manor house and resident lord.

Except for a few cases sent to the Devon and Exeter Hospital, people who fell ill stayed at home to recover or die there. Medicine and surgery had made great advances during the 18th century but the records made sad reading. Families were decimated by infectious diseases, smallpox and typhoid were still killers, and tuberculosis was rampant. Cholera was a constant fear: epidemics on the Continent were watched as they approached and receded from the Channel ports. Memorials in the church record the deaths of young people who came here for the sea air, which was believed to be beneficial for TB sufferers, but after long illnesses they died here.

In common with burial grounds across the country, the churchyards of the district were becoming full by the middle of the 19th century. So a Burial Board of nine members was formed for Sidmouth in 1877, including the Vicar, Peter Orlando Hutchinson and Major Hicks – agent for the Lord of the Manor. It was agreed to purchase three acres of land off Temple Street that had been part of the Carslake Estate and erect a pair of chapels and a lodge at an anticipated cost of £2,500. The new cemetery was consecrated on 16th December 1878 and the first two burials took place on 19th January 1879. Further land purchases took place as the town grew and demand for burial space increased, with extensions opened in 1911, 1958 and 2004. The allotments adjacent to the cemetery are planned to provide further burial space in the future.

May Cottage, Sidmouth's first hospital
drawn from Nature on stone by G. Rowe, printed by P. Simonau pubd. by J. Wallis 1826

May Cottage was first used as a hospital in 1885. Funds for the new Victoria Cottage Hospital in 1889 were helped by a legacy of half the estate of the Rev. Olmius Morgan. There had been a scandal and court case in the past concerning this cleric, his wife and a servant girl. When funds were needed for the hospital's maintenance, the Kenneth Balfour family presented two evenings of tableaux vivants at Knowle.

Dr. Jeffery, "a clever and sensible surgeon", declared Sidmouth well-water contaminated and wanted water to be brought from Cotmaton springs. He was surely right especially for the low-lying parts of the town and the Marsh. There was an indignant outcry from residents who had individual wells and pumps; everyone else had to carry all supplies from a few public wells. The coming of the water and sewage mains was an important innovation. So too was gas which was installed early by P.O.H. in September 1864. When gas lighting was brought to the church there were complaints about the glare.

In 1887, Sidmouth, like the rest of Britain celebrated Queen Victoria's Golden Jubilee with great enthusiasm and many memorials. In 1897, the crowned heads of all Europe came to London for her Diamond Jubilee. In January 1901 she died at Osborne House after a short illness. Britain seemed unthinkable without her.

THE 20th CENTURY –
A CENTURY OF CHANGE

Sidmouth, like the rest of England, entered the 20th century twice; once when the calendar changed and again thirteen months later when the old Queen died. At the time it was widely believed that the accession of Edward VII would inaugurate a period of peace, prosperity and gaiety. In retrospect we can see that it undoubtedly marked the beginning of great economic, social and political changes. Sidmouth was not exempt from these changes, although a few may have been somewhat delayed.

In 1900 Sidmouth's High Street was still residential rather than commercial. Elegant houses of the town's doctors stood where M&Co. and bank buildings are found today. But there were, also, a number of modest thatched cottages, some of which were pulled down as late as 1932 to make way for the Gas Showrooms and what were then a garage and the Fire Station – all now gone. The thatched buildings of Church Street were destroyed by fire in December 1927, and in 1929 the old Market House was demolished and replaced by the one that stands today. At the top of the town, the cinema and the former main Post Office rose where new estates were opening up by pulling down the Vicarage and the old thatched house of Radway. To the west, 1900 saw the cutting of the first sod to make the Bickwell Valley road. In 1900 the fields began at Radway, and Kelly's Directory of 1902 describes Woolbrook as a "straggling hamlet one mile from the town". Woolbrook continued to grow and following a meeting in August 1927 when the building of a new church was discussed and agreed, Col. Balfour, Lord of the Manor, gave the land for a church to hold 250 people, laying the foundation stone in December 1929. Stone was provided from the reopened Dunscombe quarry from which, in earlier centuries, stone had been used for Exeter Cathedral, and Sidbury, Sidmouth and Salcombe Regis churches. The new church, St. Francis of Assisi, was consecrated by the Lord Bishop of Exeter in January 1938.

Sidmouth was a fishing village in the 18th and 19th centuries and in 1900 some 23 drifters still worked from stations ranged from Fort Cottage in the west, along the Esplanade to the east by the Lifeboat Slip at the top of Ham Lane. By 1907 only seven boats remained in service, for Sidmouth had not escaped the rapid decline of Britain's inshore fisheries as they succumbed to competition from the industrialized trawling and drift-netting. Additionally, Britain lost not only a supply of fresh fish but also an invaluable source of skilled recruits for the Royal Naval Reserve in which many Sidmouth fishermen's families played their part. Tribute must be paid to the fishermen who over the centuries were the mainstay of the town, some of whose descendants are still with us today. The 'William and Frances', like the 'Rimington' which she replaced, was an open lifeboat rowed by its crew and launched directly over the shingle beach on a wheeled carriage. Fortunately, so few calls were made on her services, largely as a result of the move from sail to steam, that in 1912 it proved possible to concentrate the RNLI lifeboat service in Exmouth.

Today, fishing contributes almost nothing to the economy of the town. Instead, Sidmouth has become a seaside holiday resort for those who appreciate the friendliness of its shops and hotels and the restraint which has preserved its seafront from exploitation by the noisy, gaudy amusements and garish shops of brasher promenades. In 1953 the Automobile Association Handbook listed four 4-star and four 3-star hotels for Sidmouth; only six towns in England had more.

Doubtless because they are more than usually rational, Sidmouth has attracted eminent scientists in their retirement. Sir Norman Lockyer, FRS, was famous as the astronomer who discovered helium in the sun; he was also the founder-editor of the scientific journal 'Nature' and in 1912 he built the observatory on Salcombe Hill. The prolific electrical inventor S. G. Brown, FRS, bought the house built by Lady Lockyer and renamed it Brownlands. Sir Ambrose Fleming, FRS, inventor of the thermionic valve that made radio possible, lived in the town. Professor Lindemann, FRS, later Viscount Cherwell whose early life was at Sidholme in Elysian Fields, became Winston Churchill's scientific adviser during the Second World War.

A number of well-known authors have had links with Sidmouth. H. G. Wells was sufficiently impressed with the local scenery to locate his short story 'The Sea Raiders' around Jacob's Ladder. Beatrix Potter visited the town in April 1898 and spent six family holidays here, the last in 1908, and painted a view of its beach and cliffs. She also sketched the local buildings and landscape and set part of the

Stephen Reynolds and the Woolleys, 1908
L to R, "Punch", Sam, "Chip", Tom, Stephen Reynolds, Bob

'Tale of Little Pig Robinson' in Salcombe Regis and the Sid Valley; 'Stymouth' is Sidmouth. Stephen Reynolds who called Sidmouth 'Seacombe'. In his novel 'A Poor Man's House,' which was published in 1908, he provides a moving and graphic account of the life of the local fisherman Bob Woolley and his family with whom the author lived and worked. R. F. Delderfield wrote many books and plays, and was well-known and well-liked as a resident over many years.

Many visitors, also, have decided to take out a season ticket and retire here. This, too, changed the nature of the town as services, accommodation, leisure activities and numerous societies developed to suit an above average proportion of older people. However, despite the superior longevity of woman, the sex ratio in Sidmouth remained close to two men to three women throughout the century.

It would be tedious to attempt to chronicle in detail the many steps by which Sidmouth grew from 1,300 houses and 5,800 inhabitants in the census year 1901 to more than 3,000 houses and 10,000 inhabitants in 1951 and to almost 12,500 inhabitants by 1981. Suffice it to say that whereas, between 1901 and 1981, the population of Devon increased by 44%, as against 51% for England and Wales, Sidmouth's increase was 114%. A comparison of the town plans for 1885 and 1985 gives a vivid impression of rapid and sustained growth, most of which occurred in Woolbrook and Sidford during the century.

Education for the infant and junior inhabitants of Sidmouth covered a wide spectrum from Church and National schools to Council schools and private schools. The story is too complex to be told here but the development of secondary education deserves more than a passing mention. Sidmouth College has provided sixth-form courses to A-level since 1982. It had previously offered teaching to CSE and O-level as a Secondary Modern School; and before moving to its new purpose-built premises in Primley Road in 1965 it had occupied what is now St. Nicholas Primary School at Woolbrook. In earlier years this had been an elementary Council school covering all ages up to fourteen.

To a visitor, Sidmouth still retained an old-world air, even though Theophilus (Toff) Mortimore no longer peacocked resplendent in knee breeches and cocked hat to cry around the town of things lost and found and of more portentous matters beside. Certainly the town's character altered considerably. In 1900 it was being commended as a health resort for the old and sickly, as in the 18th and 19th centuries it had been regarded as a "fashionable watering place" for the wealthy – meaning not a spa, but a place for sea-water baths and bathing.

The Sidmouth Bath Company was one of several private ventures launched by the energetic agents of the Lord of the Manor. The baths, located on the Esplanade, were used by the Red Cross in the 1914-18 war to treat wounded officers but, such are the vagaries of medical fashion, they fell into a fatal decline with the rise of more convenient forms of electrical treatment which did not involve the costs of heating water or the chore of digging shingle out of the intake pipe on the beach. They closed in 1935.

In the last century, the mores of Sidmouth changed beyond recognition. Beach attire was decorous, even formal, in 1900; bathing machines were still in use and voluminous bathing costumes concealed much more than they revealed. Valetudinarians in bath chairs were pushed sedately along the front by paid nurses or companions and outwardly respectable fishermen rowed and sailed visitors around the bay. Beach pyjamas appeared in the 1930s and as the century progressed the squeamish were grateful for any costume, however exiguous. Men, though, bathed nude on Western Beach in 1900.

The streets themselves altered greatly for there was no tarmac in 1900. In winter they lay deep in mud and in summer carts moved around spraying water to lay the dust. The roadway was made of cracked flints bonded with clay and more or less flattened with a horse-drawn roller. Horses also pulled the tradesmen's delivery vans, the gentlefolk's carriages, the hand-pumped fire engine, hotel omnibuses and Alfred Dean's little droshkies that plied for hire. Mr. Hodges introduced the first motor taxi in 1911, but the trains it and the droshkies went to meet were axed by Beeching in 1967. Horse-drawn transport has its own peculiar forms of pollution and each summer the town's Surveyor was urged to clear away the municipal manure dump on the Bedford Lawn at more frequent intervals in view of the accumulating evidence of its proximity to the Esplanade.

When the 20th century dawned there were few motor cars in Sidmouth but their number increased greatly after about 1912. It was, no doubt, their superior dust-raising speed and their tender pneumatic tyres that led to the tarring which began in Fore Street in 1912 and was applied more generally in the 1920s. So began the shift of Sidmouth's road problems from dust and mud to parking and congestion: driving in Sidmouth was always very much a middle-of-the road affair, without undue bias to left or right! The streets were the responsibility of the Sidmouth Urban District Council (SUDC). The Council had come into being only six years before 1900 and struggled at first to find its feet in the face of an alternative source of power and influence already well-established in the town. That source was 'The Manor'. As traffic increased, a one-way system was introduced in the 1970s. The old gas works which had been built on part of the Ham in the 19th century was finally demolished after World War II and the site turned into a large car park. Later other old buildings were demolished to extend it further. The old archery field close to Jacobs Ladder was bought by SUDC from the owner of Peak House and also made into a car park serving Jacobs Ladder beach.

The Manor of Sidmouth had been inherited by John Edmund Heugh Balfour who as a young man joined the 11th Hussars and served with distinction in the Boer and the 1914-18 wars, rising in military rank and honour to become Col. J. E. H. Balfour CMG, DSO. When the century began, the Lord of the Manor was 37 years old, and he was assisted by two very effective agents – W. H. Hastings, his solicitor, and R. W. Sampson, his architect. Between them they changed the face of Sidmouth. In those days, many things that we now expect some public authority to perform were initiated and steered by the Manor. The Sidmouth Water Co. had arisen from Col. Balfour's concern about the insanitary wells in the town; but he had been resisted by strongly conservative Sidmouthians who professed themselves happy with the water their fathers had drunk and who saw no reason why a new-fangled, and more expensive, piped-water system should be foisted on them by the Manor. Some felt this so strongly that the works at Sidbury were attacked and damaged and had to be guarded.

Mr. Hastings, on behalf of the Manor, was either the secretary or a director of the Sidmouth Bath Co., the Sidmouth Gas Co., the Sidmouth Railway Co., and the Sidmouth Hotels Co. which designed

Victoria Hotel opening in 1904

and built the Victoria – the only purpose-built hotel in Sidmouth. In the early part of the century the tide of political opinion ran strongly against what was called 'municipal trading' which the more affluent feared would lay a burden on the rates. It was into these unpropitious times that the infant local authorities had been born to deal with the risks to health and the environmental nuisances caused by those unpopular and unprofitable items – the sewers. Where their interests met, conflicts developed between the Council and the Manor, as two examples will show.

In pursuit of their duty to improve Sidmouth's ill-made roads, the Council decided to replace their horse-drawn roller with a much heavier steam model. Unfortunately its weight cracked the gas and water mains which, economically rather than prudently, the companies had laid a mere 9 to 12 inches below the road surface of poorly-consolidated flints. As the Secretary of both Companies, Mr. Hastings waxed eloquent and even threatened to issue writs to restrain the Council. The Council, stung, retorted that the gas supply was low in quality as it was in pressure. It also criticised the cost and effectiveness of the gas street lamps – not surprisingly, since naked gas jets were used to save the cost of incandescent mantles and, as a further economy, the lamps were turned off for three days before and after each full moon.

The second example relates to the beach. The Lord of the Manor believed himself to have rights over the foreshore and he removed substantial quantities of shingle for his own purposes; moreover he levied a charge of 2d a load on others who took shingle to make concrete or as a top-dressing for roads and paths. Around 1905 to 1908 the level of the beach was low enough to worry the fishermen and their spokesman Stephen Reynolds noted in a letter that: "Thousands of loads go in a year… it's going to be no joke to fight the all-powerful manor". A public enquiry was held and in December 1908 the Board of Trade issued an order prohibiting the taking of shingle from the Town Beach on penalty of a £10 fine. In careful anticipation, several hundred tons had been removed each week and stored in pits and yards. The Manor lost little more than prestige for, as W. H. Hastings commented to Stephen Reynolds, the prohibition order "had put a thousand a year into the Lord of the Manor's pocket from his flint quarries". The situation was not tidied up until 1937 when the Council acquired the foreshore from the Board of Trade.

At the enquiry, R. W. Sampson had given evidence that 8,695 tons of shingle had been removed over the previous 17 years – a curiously exact figure and certainly far too low. Its shingle beach is low-lying Sidmouth's front-line defence against flooding by the sea. Unfortunately it tends to be low in stormy periods and then the sea-wall is exposed to the full force of the waves. Exceptionally severe weather in 1924 washed away the shingle, the sea-wall was breached and the town was flooded. Only three years earlier a substantial sum had been applied to sea defence works but by 20th March 1926 a further £69,000 had been spent in refacing the wall along the whole length of the Esplanade with a stone apron 23ft high and 8ft thick, built on foundations dug 3ft deep into the underlying sandstone. The sea-wall was then secure, but the Esplanade had lost a tall landmark – The Big Lamp by the York steps which had been lit each night as a beacon for returning fishermen. The Ministry of Transport contributed £16,000, Devon County Council £15,000, and the town had to borrow £38,000 to finance the balance.

At the end of the 1914-18 war, much of the Manor property was sold to its sitting tenants and, when Col. Balfour died in October 1952, the Council bought the residue of the estate together with the title. The Council's undisputed reign was, however, short-lived: in 1974, the reconstruction of local government transferred most of its powers and responsibilities to a new District Council covering the whole of East Devon, and the Town Council declined to the status of a parish forum. By this act Sidmouth's affairs were much diluted, becoming one small component of a large and wide-ranging agenda over which its representatives exercise only a minority vote.

Speaking towards the end of his life, Col. Balfour regretted that the town had always been suspicious of the Manor and often, in his view, unreasonably opposed to its schemes for improvements from which, although the Manor would not have lost, the town would certainly have gained. It was his misfortune to live at the end of an era when feudal patronage, however benevolent, was certain to be opposed. Privilege had for too long reaped its advantages and the new men were bound to flex their muscles.

In fact, Sidmouth owes much both to its Town Council and to the last Lord of its Manor. As well as his initiative in the various commercial ventures already mentioned, Col. Balfour built the Manor Hall, developed Bickwell Valley and gave many plots of land for public use – for example, Manstone Meadow, Glen Goyle and part of the Three-cornered Plot, also known as The Triangle. He had given land to extend the Cottage Hospital and he offered land for Council houses, allotments and a library. He also released other key sites for sale, including the Cricket Field and the Golf Course. Col. Balfour was the principal but he was not the only private benefactor. Thus, Sir Clive Morrison Bell had purchased and given to the town in 1924 the field now held in trust for use by the Rugby Club. Among many other benefactors was Miss Leigh Browne who in 1937 handed over some 20 acres of land in the Byes to the National Trust to maintain as an open space for ever.

In 1914, the Town Council purchased the Blackmore Hall estate for £4,400 and opened the Coburg Field portion of it in 1922 for tennis, bowling and croquet. The old house decayed and was demolished and, on 18th July 1953, its grounds were opened as the Blackmore Gardens. In 1930 the Council bought Mr. Jemmett's house 'Sea View' for £3,500; that house also was pulled down and its grounds were developed into public gardens – Connaught Gardens – opened and named by the Duke of Connaught on 3rd November 1934. The lighting of the Esplanade was improved in 1952 by erecting distinctive, tall lamp standards of Iroko wood and in 1953 the Council bought the Manor Hall. The lamp standards were replaced in the early 21st century due to the warping and twisting of the timber over the years. The replacements were similar in appearance but made of metal.

As well as providing these and other amenities, the Town Council acquired the Gas Works in 1912 and, in 1940, to improve the eastern end of the Esplanade, moved them at considerable expense, from the Ham to a site near the railway station. These buildings were not demolished until after World War II when a new gas main was laid from Exeter to supply Sidmouth. The Council also built and operated an electricity generating station whose diesel-driven dynamo began to supply direct current in 1926; the engine shed and battery house were demolished and became part of a car park. The

Council handled the major reconstruction of the sea wall in 1925-6, bought the Water Works in 1933, and, after many years of debate, acquired land and built council housing estates of several hundred houses.

No account of the twentieth century should avoid mentioning its three major wars – the South African, the 1914-18, and the 1939-45. Sidmouth played its part in each of these. It knew its griefs, and staged its celebrations, and in each war made a contribution which was thoroughly creditable but not distinctively different in kind or quantity from those of other Devon towns of similar size.

In Sidmouth, the outbreak of war in August 1914 came as a shock. The local fishermen were mostly Navy reservists, so were called up immediately, while many of the remaining men joined up in the first few months of the conflict. As in other parts of the country, it fell to the young, the old and the women to keep life going. The Linen League was quickly organised, providing clothing and hospital necessaries for the front. The first Belgian refugees arrived in November and troops were billeted in the town from December – occupying many of the available halls, together with Church House (now Kennaway House) which suffered considerable damage from its use by the Territorial Cyclists, due to excess weight on the upper floors. The first Sidmouth losses came in November when HMS Monmouth was lost in the naval battle of Coronel off Chile. The captain was a friend of Stephen Reynolds, author of A Poor Man's House, who gave up his writing to spend the war organising the inshore fisheries of southwest England. In June, the town was alive with pomp and ceremony for a visit by the recruiting officer but, as in other East Devon towns, the success rate was small – those who were going to join had already done so. From the start, the town tried to publish the names of those who had enlisted. However, as time went on, the emphasis shifted to the casualties. From the latter part of 1916, neighbourhood shrines were set up recording those from the surrounding streets who had enlisted and those who had been killed. Eventually over sixteen such shrines were erected, each flying a Union Jack and flanked by flowers. The sinking of food convoys in May 1917 resulted in food shortages in the whole country, and Sidmouth was subject to the King's proclamation to reduce consumption, especially of bread. Around this time, the church curate joined up as a chaplain and his letters, reprinted in the parish magazine, provide a vivid picture of life in the trenches of northern France. November 1918 brought the end of the war – the church bells rang from 11am and the church and churchyard quickly filled with townspeople celebrating the armistice. The memorial to those who were killed was erected in 1921 to a design by R. W. Sampson, consisting of a Celtic cross in the churchyard, and two marble tablets listing the 117 names of the fallen inside the church tower, beneath the Queen's window. The old curate's house opposite became the Sidmouth War Memorial Club for Ex-Servicemen.

In World War II the seafront was barricaded with barbed wire and scaffolding, with little access allowed to the beach. Concrete 'tank trap' pyramids blocked access to the seafront from the market and Clifton slipway where a life-like imitation cottage housed a gun. There were additional tank traps all along the shingle beach just below the tide-line. On the lower field at Peak Hill were gun emplacements, one being at the top of Jacob's Ladder. A pill box has been retained there as a memorial to 389 Coastal Battery RA. Bickwell Farm received bomb damage and Salcombe Regis Church had the south windows blown out.

Army and Royal Air Force contingents were stationed in the town and 3949 official evacuees were accepted, mostly from London, in addition to many others staying privately in guest houses and unrequisitioned parts of hotels.

Following the 1939-45 war an inscription was added to the War Memorial and a tablet to that of their comrades of 1914-18 in the church. Arcot House, near Exeter Cross, originally the seat of General Lumley, was purchased and renovated as a residential home for elderly people and became the town's memorial to those who lost their lives in World War II.

TOWARDS 2000

The 20th century carried Sidmouth from Edwardian opulence, with its sharp – and often painful – class distinctions, to 1990's more democratic days. From bathing machines to bikinis. From paddle-steamer trips (which ended abruptly in 1934 when the Duchess of Devonshire ran aground on the beach at Port Royal and was broken up) to wind surfing. From cheap day excursions by rail from Waterloo to coach trips and congested car parks. From seasonal bands and pierrots on the Esplanade and a sand artist on the beach to the Sidmouth International Festival of Folk Arts. From amateur concerts, and the birth and heyday of the cinema, to radio and television. From Sabbath observance to Sunday trading.

The seafront saw the most change. In 1921, work on the Esplanade included a 45cm wall which would reduce flooding of the road in times of high seas. Peak Hill Road beyond Connaught Gardens rises to over 91 metres over the sea and in January 1936 a 55 metre stretch of the road and adjoining land out to the cliff collapsed and a new road was built further inland. Sixty years later, in January 1996, part of the road again collapsed and a new re-routed

The Duchess of Devonshire high and dry on Sidmouth beach in 1934

section was constructed. Similar collapses happened on Salcombe Hill, forcing the closure of a section of a much loved footpath, and necessitating a loop via Cliff Road.

As a protection from coastal erosion, new offshore defences were commenced in 1994 in the form of two bouldered islands at the western end of the Esplanade. Along the beach, rock reinforcement breakwaters replaced the wooden groynes in an attempt to retain the shingle. In 1992, most of the shingle was swept away, scouring down to bedrock along the main seafront. Rocks which had not been seen in living memory appeared, and the keel and rudder of the Duchess of Devonshire were uncovered. Over the next two years many tons of quarry pebbles were brought in by fleets of lorries to prevent further encroachment of the sea. Railings were installed along the edge of the promenade as a safety measure in case of future lowering of the beach. In 1999 a locally-funded millennium project, 'The Clifton Walkway', was completed and resulted in a continuous walkway linking the Esplanade to the Jacob's Ladder beach.

Clifton Walkway – photo: Reg Lane

Fishing continued in a small way at Port Royal with boats operated by the Bagwell family, despite the difficulties of working from an ever changing shingle beach. Nearby are the premises of the Inshore Rescue Service and the Sailing Club Headquarters. Alongside, on the Ham, a new building completed in December 1991 accommodates the swimming pool and the Tourist Information Centre.

Tourism was still the main support of the town despite the closure of the railway station and branch line in 1967. Visitors arrived by car and coach for day trips and longer stays. Larger hotels have survived the changes in holiday patterns, but many of the smaller ones and guesthouses were converted to flats, self-catering apartments, holiday homes or returned to being homes in permanent occupation.

A chineway constructed at Jacob's Ladder in 1963 provides easier access to the beach. Nearby, the Connaught Gardens offered a riot of colour in the summer, and various entertainments take place in

Jacob's Ladder and chineway – photo: Andrew Rugg-Gunn

the delightful surroundings, including holiday season concerts by the Town Band, and performances by local and visiting theatre groups. A popular addition was the cafe in the Old Clock Tower building, well-known to those walking the SW Coast Path. Within the town, the Blackmore Gardens and adjoining Bowling Greens offered other quiet places in which to relax.

Sidmouth Town Band concert in Connaught Gardens

The first cinema, the Belle Vue, opened in 1913 in Fore Street in premises now occupied by Fat Face, a clothing shop. It was replaced by two cinemas – the Grand in High Street operated from 1929 until 1956 when it was destroyed by fire, and the site became shops and the St John Hall. The new Radway Theatre opened in June 1928, with a musical production. In the following year talking pictures were becoming the rage and were introduced in December that year. The Radway continued as a cinema – a valuable amenity for a town this size.

The town enjoyed extra publicity in 1987/88 and 1990 when visiting television and film crews were making 'Vanity Fair', 'A Summer Story' and 'Jeeves and Wooster'.

The Manor Pavilion provided live entertainment by a professional repertory company from July to September. At other times, the hall was in frequent use when local amateur groups performed plays, musicals and concerts as well as being the prime location for talks and meetings by many local organisations.

In early August 1955, the English Folk Dance and Song Society came to the town to perform. That small event grew over 40 years to be an annual highlight of the holiday period at the beginning of August, and was renamed The Sidmouth International Festival of Folk Arts. Performers come from all over the world to take part.

The field adjoining the Belmont Hotel was bought in 1935 and this beautiful site became home to the Sidmouth Cricket, Lawn Tennis and Croquet Club, which celebrated its 175th anniversary in 1998. Beneath its southern boundary, shelters facing out to sea were constructed in 1938 to seat about 100 people.

The shopping area of the town was mainly unchanged, apart from the town enhancement scheme of pedestrianised red brick paved areas and black street furniture. Shop frontages altered in some cases, but most retained their original upper storeys – for example the London Hotel and its livery stables which stood at the junction of Fore and New Street, are now shops. Trumps in Fore Street retained its original frontage and maintained its reputation as a high class grocery (but closed in 2014 after 200 years).

The Sidmouth Parish Church of St Giles and St Nicholas (the latter being the patron saint of sailors) was given a new weather vane in 1992. It was commissioned by Peter Rose in memory of his wife Margaret whom he had met near the church in 1947. Designed by an artist-blacksmith and family friend, Lennox Kilner, it takes the form of the 'Mary Rose', the famous Tudor warship, and bears Mrs. Rose's initials MJR on its gilded sail. Below the ship is a pennant-shaped part of the old vane, which had long seized up, dated 1809.

Over a period of 125 years Sidmouth, had three breweries but the last one ceased production in 1957. The site was redeveloped with houses and flats, but the name Brewery Lane is retained.

Sidmouth Urban District Council (SUDC) was created in 1894 but it was not until 1921 that it moved into its first permanent office in Castle House, High Street. In 1929 this house was sold and the Grand Cinema was built on its site. A local resident, Miss Constance Radford gave the Council permission to occupy Hope Cottage at the top of Church Street. In 1936 the Council moved again, this time into nearby Norton Garth, and Hope Cottage became the public library.

The SUDC's last move came in 1968 when it bought the Knowle Hotel and converted the accommodation into offices to suit the needs of a growing town but, six years later the local government reforms of 1974 saw the Council's demise. The new East Devon District Council (EDDC) took on most of the UDC's responsibilities and the remainder were handed to the newly created Sidmouth Town Council, which moved into Woolcombe House. The Coat of Arms, which had been received by Sidmouth Urban District Council in 1964, was handed over to the Town Council and the library vellum paintingof the Arms now hangs in the Council Chamber.

The EDDC had responsibilities for over 120,000 people and became the town's largest employer. Eight of the sixty elected members represent the Sidmouth area.

In 1994, a reception was held at Knowle to celebrate one hundred years of local government. The EDDC presented the Town Council with a Commemorative Deed, framed and printed on vellum, which assigned to the Town Council, the Lordship of the Manor of Sidmouth, a title rooted in Anglo-Saxon England before 1066.

In the late 1960s, Cherry Hayes, a house near the hospital, was for sale. It was sold, demolished and in its place the Health Centre and new Devon County Library were built and opened in 1970. This enabled the transfer of the museum from Woolcombe House to Hope Cottage – so it was all change! The Museum was incorporated with the Sid Vale Heritage Centre to encompass more activities.

Sidmouth's Victoria Cottage Hospital, which opened in 1885, changed much during the next 100 years. More major upgrading schemes in various parts of the hospital were undertaken in 1990, 1992 and 1998 costing in all £1.5 million, paid for by the generosity of local people to the Hospital Comforts Fund. The 1998 alterations cost £800,000 and the new facilities were opened by Her Royal Highness the Princess Royal in February 1999. We now have a modern community hospital and 'Cottage' has been dropped from the title.

The Sid Vale Association, since its formation in 1846 'for the enhancement and preservation of the Sid Valley' did just that and continues to do so. In partnership with local authorities, it maintained some 50 miles of footpaths and bridleways. Together with the National Trust it preserved the Byes, 20 acres of which were given by Annie Leigh-Browne in 1937, as a public open space and peaceful riverside walk from the town to Sidford. In 1986 it again linked up with the National Trust in the successful 'Landscape Appeal' to save forever the summits of Salcombe Hill and Peak Hill from being spoilt by development. This comprised 20 acres of Peak Hill and 200 acres on Salcombe Hill. The Trust now own the coast from Sidmouth to Branscombe and on to Beer Head. The town raised £220,000 to buy the 220 acres in 1985/6. The achievement was commemorated with a visit by Her Royal Highness the Duchess of Kent in September 1986. Support of the Sid Vale Association has continued and membership reached 3000 in 1998.

The Observatory on Salcombe Hill, extended in 1995, was now managed by the Norman Lockyer Observatory Society and has facilities for optical astronomy, meteorology, radio communications and satellite studies of the Earth. It attracted numerous educational visits and courses to meet the ever growing interest in its activities.

The Duchess of Kent with Sir Jack Boles, Chairman of the Landscape Appeal Committee – photo courtesy of Sidmouth Museum

EARLY YEARS IN THE NEW MILLENNIUM

Sidmouth's important events in the first part of the century have been very broadly concerned with the tension between conservation and development although one is not exclusive of the other. As will be seen, the Sid Vale Association (SVA) has been especially central in a period of extraordinary activity in which various groups have been formed to enrich the town for both residents and visitors of all ages.

About 4000 people gathered in festive mood on the Esplanade on New Year's Eve 1999 to welcome the new millennium. In November 2012 a similar number again assembled in the same location but on this occasion the mood was anything but celebratory. SOS (Save Our Sidmouth) was formed earlier that year and consisted, amongst others, of representatives of the SVA, the Chamber of Commerce and the Hospitality Association. It fiercely opposed the proposals of the East Devon District Council (EDDC) to firstly establish a 12 acre employment site at Sidford and secondly to sell their headquarters at the Knowle and move away from the town with likely job loss and irreversible loss of parkland, previously accessible to the public. The Council's rationale for relocation was that there was a requirement for modern, efficient offices to offer

SOS protesters march to the Knowle – Photo: Sidmouth Herald

best value to the taxpayers rather than the present site which was an unsatisfactory hotel conversion. SOS attempted unsuccessfully to have the site listed by English Heritage who turned down the application indicating that the building and parkland, although of interest, had already been extensively developed and little of the original landscape was preserved. Feelings ran high and in November 2012 possibly as many as 4000 protesters marched from the Esplanade up Station Road to the Knowle, reflecting the widespread anger of many of the citizens with the EDDC proposals. The initial EDDC plan was a move to Skypark outside Exeter but in 2014 the proposal was a split location site between a new build in Honiton and redevelopment of Exmouth Town Hall, whilst the Knowle site would be redeveloped as a retirement community.

In May 2015 the citizens of Sidmouth won a pyrrhic victory in the Council election when 'independents', including members of the newly formed East Devon Alliance, ousted those Tory incumbents who supported relocation.

The Fortfield Hotel was another controversial development scheme. The 1891 private house, The Red House, had been enlarged by Sampson in 1902 as a hotel and was of architectural interest rather than great beauty. Nevertheless there was a general fondness for it. In the mid-2000s planning applications to modernise the hotel were rejected on several occasions and the condition of the empty building worsened. In late 2010 and early 2011 it was extensively damaged by fire which, on the second occasion, threatened to spread to the nearby newly thatched cricket pavilion. The old Fortfield was subsequently demolished and a new hotel was anticipated. Instead, and contrary to the wishes of the business community, there is a development of 29 apartments. It has been named Sanditon after the title of Jane Austen's unfinished final novel which describes a fictitious town, Sanditon, which may be based on Sidmouth. It is a satire about property development speculation in a seaside resort in the early 19th century and the author would have appreciated the irony of history repeating itself.

Some old buildings have been replaced by something altogether more satisfactory. In the last century, the gloomy Sea View, at the foot of Peak Hill, was demolished and the attractive Connaught

Gardens created. The decrepit Blackmore Hall was replaced by the peaceful Blackmore Gardens. The case of Church House, however, is instructive as it combined conservation with innovation. This fine Georgian building twice came back from the brink of being demolished. It was built in 1805 and named Fort House as the western aspect faced the small fort in what is now Fortfield, the site of the cricket ground. Towards the end of the 19th century the house fell into disrepair but was rescued in 1905 by Richard Wood. He ensured that the parish church had a centre for social activities and accordingly Fort House was renamed Church House. During the Great War the building again deteriorated. It was requisitioned for the use of Territorial Cyclists who inadvertently caused a floor to collapse. A further decline in its fortune continued through the 20th century and it was close to demolition and redevelopment when, in 2004, a large grant from the Heritage Lottery Fund, combined with generous contributions from other charitable funds as well as from both the Town and East Devon District Councils, saved the building. In 2007 the Sidmouth Herald invited the general public to decide between 'Fort', 'Church' and 'Kennaway' as an appropriate name

Kennaway House – Photo: *John Dowell*

for the extensively renovated building and the ballot favoured Kennaway House. The Kennaways were important residents in the early 19th century although, strictly speaking, the first owner was Captain Thomas Phillipps. The official opening was on July 4th 2009, and the venue is used for art exhibitions, adult and community learning, guest lectures, jazz concerts and literary festivals.

In 2001, the Jurassic Coast (Dorset and East Devon) became England's first natural World Heritage Site. The 95 mile coastline includes, of course, this town (the distinctive red cliffs are from the Triassic rather than the Jurassic era). In 2011 the seafront arches on the western Esplanade were renovated and include a Jurassic Coast Interpretation Centre which describes both the surrounding countryside and coast, and the South West Coastal Path. The Jurassic Coast Partnership also provided the Museum with interpretation displays. Fortuitously, Triassic vertebrate fossilised footprints were found below High Peak and at Pennington Point and donated to the Museum collection.

The Jurassic Coast Team writes that this World Heritage Site is "...beautiful and interesting and internationally important because it is eroding". The inevitable consequence of this coastal erosion,

Erosion of Cliff Road properties – Photo: Sidmouth Herald

specifically at Pennington Point (the cliffs east of the mouth of the Sid) is the danger to properties on Cliff Road. Residents formed an action group explaining that their land is disappearing at a rate of about 4 metres a year and therefore a rock retaining wall, running along the base of the cliff, was urgently required. Others have argued that the cliff erosion is due to water seepage from the top and such a wall would be ineffective. The conflict between coastal protection and natural erosion continues but any scheme has to receive approval from Natural England. The town itself is protected from flooding by sea walls, rock groynes and offshore rock breakwaters, but these may have contributed to low beach levels and possibly to the eastern cliff erosion. There is a perennial problem of loss of shingle from the beach and a century ago it was one of the factors that hastened the demise of the fishing trade. Another casualty of these natural processes has been Alma Bridge. The original bridge was built in 1855 but, after sea and storm damage, was replaced in 1900 by a wooden bridge on brick piers designed by Sampson. A new, third bridge is planned for 2016 which will incorporate some of Sampson's original work. Flood and wind damage was exceptionally severe in November 2012 when the town was cut off by water for several hours and the Byes submerged. Storms in 2014 again resulted in the roads into the town being blocked but this time it was due to fallen trees. Beach huts at Jacob's Ladder were destroyed and over 100 tonnes of shingle and debris had to be removed from the hard-standing at Jacob's Ladder and Esplanade.

Stormy seas destroying beach huts at Jacob's Ladder – Photo: *John Dowell*

In 2005, partly in response to the anticipated increase in tourism after achieving 'Jurassic Coast' status, the Vision Group for Sidmouth was formed. It was the idea of the then chairman of the SVA, the Reverend Handel Bennett, with a general aim of improving local amenities. Interesting proposals included a major cultural centre at Port Royal, better access to the town with a Park & Ride

scheme, a footbridge to connect the Manor Car Park and Connaught Gardens, and a pier or jetty to improve access for boats. Whilst there was general support for these initial schemes there has been, to date, little progress. There have been, however, notable later successful and important initiatives including SidEnergy (a community energy cooperative), the annual Climate Week and Sidmouth Science Festival.

An important attraction remains the Museum located in the Regency building, Hope Cottage. The displays, many of which are changed from season to season, include a wide range of subjects, mainly local; from Sidmouth's famous scientists to Sidmouth's own campervan; from 19th century prints to a 19th century printing press, and very many more. Perhaps the most treasured item is Hubert Cornish's panoramic watercolour, 'The Long Picture'. The three preparatory sketches for this painting were an exciting 2013 acquisition. Dr Bob Symes, who became Curator in 2001 and initiated free admission in 2009, has seen the visitor figures increase from 5,000 to 13,000 per year.

One of three preparatory sketches for the Long Picture in Sidmouth Museum

In 1985-6 Margaret Clark persuaded the SVA and the National Trust to launch the Landscape Appeal. Some of the money, augmented by a generous legacy, enabled the purchase, in 2002, of farmland, named Margaret's Meadow a year later. The adjacent Gilchrist Field had already been purchased by the SVA in 1996 and these two fields add interest to walking in the Byes. In 2011 a voluntary group, the Friends of the Byes received a large lottery grant towards planting new trees, a community orchard and developing wildlife trails in this historic parkland adjacent to the river. Informative interpretation boards with maps were sited between the Toll House and Sidford. A striking attraction is the wildflower display in the upper part of Sid Meadow, now accessible to the public, having previously been fenced off and grazed by sheep. The Byes is a rich educational resource; Annie Leigh Browne, who had a lifelong interest in education and gifted Sid Meadow in 1935 to the National Trust, would have been gratified.

Other prominent philanthropists to the town include Richard Thornton who in the 19th century resurrected cricket facilities on

Margaret's Meadow – *Photo: John Dowell*

Keith Owen

the Fort Field. Numerous plots of land were given by Colonel Balfour, Lord of the Manor in the first half of the 20th century, as described in an earlier chapter. However, the one with the likeliest continuing influence is Keith Owen (1938-2007). He served 20 years in the RAF and then worked in financial services in Canada before retiring in 1986. Although Devon born, he was not a Sidmothian although he visited the town frequently as his mother lived here, describing it as "England as it used to be". When he developed a rapid, terminal illness, he decided to leave his estate, £2.3 million, to the SVA: the capital was to be a permanent endowment and the income generated was to be distributed on a regular basis to support local projects. The Keith Owen Fund (KOF) has helped a large variety of projects including a new scout headquarters, renovation of the Cricket, Tennis, Croquet and Hockey Club, purchase of the Sidmouth Hopper Bus and funding the East Devon AONB Bat Survey. The most publicised event was based on his own idea: "Plant a million bulbs! Get everyone involved". The first bulbs, daffodils, snowdrops and crocuses, were planted in autumn 2013 in 50 different sites including road-sides, park land and public gardens. It made national news and the Daily Mail banner line was "Keep Sidmouth beautiful and plant a MILLION flowers".

Another ambitious venture has been the development of Peaslands Knapp, a two acre meadow purchased by the SVA in 2010 with a footpath between Peaslands Road and the nature reserve, and maintained by volunteers. The wild flowers are mainly of the grassland variety but with some woodland species. There is a fine Turkey Oak, dating to the early 19th century, at the top of the reserve. Less usual birds such as goldcrests and redwings have been spotted. Sheep graze the meadows in the autumn. On the tithe map this area was grazed land in 1839. Small hills were called Knapp or Nap and it is possible that peas, a common crop in medieval times, were grown locally, hence Peaslands.

Some of Keith Owen's "Million Bulbs" planted above Connaught Gardens
Photo: John Dowell

Also in 2010, the Sidmouth Arboretum was launched. The imaginative idea was to create a civic arboretum to include both public and private land within the boundaries of the Town Council; this includes not only Sidmouth town but Sidford, Sidbury and Salcombe Regis, and the surrounding countryside. One major undertaking is an ongoing tree survey of the Sid Valley and already many significant trees have been mapped and descriptions are available on the Arboretum website. Other activities include talks, quizzes, Tree Trail leaflets, and guided walks with an experienced dendrologist walk leader.

Sidmouth in Bloom (SIB) has a longer civic tradition dating back to 1971. Since that time Sidmouth has won and continues to win many awards in both the South West in Bloom and the National RHS Britain in Bloom competitions. Since 2012 there has been a new direction with more emphasis on community involvement and the environment as well as hands-on gardening and gardening with children. Two recent initiatives are the Sidcombers (to help clean up the beach) and Sidbashers (to help remove Himalayan Balsam from the Sid Valley). 'Connaught Friends' are garden volunteers or guides. This continued love and care to the Connaught Gardens would have delighted John Betjeman who wrote sixty years ago: "For that is one of the first things I noticed about Sidmouth: as soon as I was out of the gentle sea breeze, I was in a hothouse where wonderful West Country bushes filled with scent and enormous butterflies lit on asters and on antirrhinums, themselves twice as large as life."

An enterprising initiative in association with the Tourist Information Centre is the Sidmouth Walking Festival. The surrounding countryside, both inland and including the South West Coast Path, makes the town an excellent centre. This annual event runs for five days in September and those taking part have a choice each day of three walks of between 4 and 11 miles in length with a walk leader. Some routes are close to the town including the Bickwell Valley, Mutters Moor and High Peak. Others are further afield including Venn Ottery, Harpford Common and Salcombe Regis.

The casual visitor to the town could be forgiven for being entirely ignorant of its fishing history. A century ago, the shingle was crowded with drifters, lobster pots and nets and there were numerous capstans for winching the vessels up the shingle. However, all is not forgotten as Sea Fest is a further annual event for all ages and its aim is to celebrate our connection with the sea in the broadest sense and also be reminded of our fishing heritage through displays, art, music and food. In his book 'All I ever wanted', Stan Bagwell, a link to the town's fishing past, describes the time when he had four boats working from the beach.

The East Devon AONB (Area of Outstanding Natural Beauty) initiated a three-year project in 2010 called 'In the Footsteps of Peter Orlando Hutchinson'. Its purpose was to raise awareness of landscape change, help conserve and enhance historical features in the Sid Valley and promote volunteer involvement in this landscape heritage. The locations were specifically those that Hutchinson had so meticulously explored and recorded in the 19th century, including High Peak, Mutters Moor and Farway Castle. Volunteers, under expert guidance, helped with scrub clearance from these historic sites. Photographs were taken of sites previously painted by Hutchinson and primary school children were taken on field trips. An interactive online 'archaeology' trail allows users to visit archaeology sites in the Sid Valley, an important resource as some are on private land.

All five volumes of Hutchinson's Diaries (1848-1894), in his spidery copperplate and some 2000 pages, were transcribed by volunteers, very much a labour of love. They are available on the East Devon AONB website as are all his watercolour paintings.

This highly productive project has contributed to the recognition that Hutchinson, arguably Sidmouth's most famous citizen, was a polymath of national importance rather than a local eccentric antiquarian who lived in a strange house with his cat and housekeeper.

AONB volunteers helping with scrub clearance

There is a long tradition of entertainment at the Manor Pavilion, originally called Manor Hall. The Sidmouth Amateur Dramatic Society (SADS) was founded in 1922. A notable production was R. F. Delderfield's (then a Sidmouth resident) 'Key of the Hut', a 1970 world premiere. In 2006 the Sidmouth Town Band joined the players for 'Brassed Off'. There are no professional productions by this society but occasionally professional actors are in the cast. In recent years the company has put on two plays and a pantomime each year. Since 1986 their headquarters and workshop have been in an attractive situation in the Byes adjacent to Lawn Vista. The Sidmouth Arts Club Operatic Society (now known as Sidmouth Musical Theatre) has a history dating back to the late 19th century and stage musical productions each spring and autumn. The Charles Vance Repertory Company had successful summer seasons from 1987 to 2013 and has been followed by the equally popular Paul Taylor-Mills Ltd.

The Sidmouth Town Band has played a major role in the life of the community for over 150 years. In Woolcombe House, the Town Council headquarters, there is an interesting 1862 photograph of the inaugural Band posed in front of the Old Chancel, then in an early stage of construction. There is a long tradition of open air Sunday evening performances from the Connaught Gardens bandstand and other regular engagements include Remembrance Day, Armed Forces Day and the Folk Festival. The Band has been to the national finals on three occasions in recent years and having progressed to the Third Section in 2008 gained further promotion to the Second Section in 2012. The Band headquarters for over 60 years have been located in the delightful thatched building adjacent to Woolcombe House but in 2015 the band chairman announced that new premises were required to allow for more equipment, a rehearsal room and, ideally, a recording studio.

The summer folk week has been an annual event since 1955. The English Folk Dance and Song Society, who started the Festival, handed over the management to a new organisation in 1987. Although the 50th Festival in 2004 was a successful and sunny week, the organisers decided not to carry on because of low financial reserves, withdrawal of investment by the EDDC and failure to secure bad weather underwriting. However, a group of enthusiasts came together to save the Festival, and they were supported by the Town

*Above, Sidmouth Steppers, the town's own women's Morris team; below, the
Sidmouth Mummers performing their traditional play, which dates back to
the Napoleonic War, during Folk Week. – Photos: John Dowell*

Council and local businesses. Because the Knowle Arena was the venue most at risk from bad weather, an enlarged marquee on the Ham replaced it as the main focus of events. The name was changed from Sidmouth International Festival to Sidmouth Folk Week, the expression used by the locals. The number of donors and sponsors has since doubled and a Supporters' Club encourages individual businesses to sponsor individual concerts.

Despite the management upheaval, Folk Week remains the most important week in the town's year, with a buzzing atmosphere and enormous goodwill. There are over 700 official Festival events including music and dance workshops as well as the main concerts. The Children's Festival, centred in Blackmore Gardens, focuses on singing, playing and crafts. Between 2010 and 2015 the number either attending or participating increased from 45,000 to 60,000. Up to 8,000 visitors come into the town each day of Folk Week. There is dancing on the Esplanade and street theatre events as well as craft stalls and varied food outlets. It is impossible to calculate accurately how much any cultural festival contributes to the local economy but for many people in both Great Britain and abroad, the name Sidmouth is associated with the Folk Festival.

In terms of numbers, even Folk Week is eclipsed by the Donkey Sanctuary at Slade House Farm. It is predicted that there will be 360,000 annual visitors by 2018. It was founded in 1969 by Elizabeth Svendsen (née Knowles) and, although initially in Ottery-St-Mary, moved to its present site close to Salcombe Regis. This location is the only one which is open to the general public but the Sanctuary is a nationwide and international organisation with 28 overseas mobile teams and 4 overseas clinics. At the Devon headquarters, which is open 365 days a year, there is especial emphasis on riding therapy for children with additional needs. It is now one of the country's leading charities and an extraordinary success story.

Slade House was the home, two centuries ago, of the affluent and influential Leigh family who, in the time of the 'Long Print', was familiar with visitors seeking cures from sea water and would have been astonished that their property should become the national centre for donkey care.

Mary King's victory parade.
Photo: Sidmouth Herald

In 2012 Weymouth hosted the Olympic sailing events, and the expert advice was that there would be a significant increase in visitors to adjacent East Devon. In the event visitor figures were disappointing but the Sid Valley citizens did have a reason to celebrate. The local equestrian sportswoman, Mary King, based near Salcombe Regis, won a Silver medal, her third medal in six Olympic Games. On August 17th, King and her horse, Imperial Cavalier, rode in a victory parade through the town, starting at the Radway, down High Street into Fore Street, onto the Esplanade and continuing up Station Road to be welcomed at Kennaway House where she was made a Freeman of the Town.

The Norman Lockyer Observatory continues to flourish and in 2006 the Donald Barber Lecture Theatre was built and the first South West Astronomy Fair was held; this is now an annual event. The following year, the Lockyer library was returned from Exeter University. In 2012, the centenary of the Observatory, the new Connaught Dome with a 20 inch reflector and the Lockyer Technology Centre were opened by the astrophysicist and rock guitarist Dr Brian May. The new dome was so called as the Duke of

The Donkey Sanctuary — Photo: John Dowell

Connaught, the third and favourite son of Queen Victoria, had opened the 1912 observatory.

Dr Brian May opening the Connaught Dome at the Lockyer Technology Centre.
Photo: Sidmouth Herald

As described in an earlier chapter, four eminent scientists, all Fellows of the Royal Society and including Norman Lockyer, lived for part of their lives in this town. The tradition lives on and modern science is reflected by the highly enterprising and very successful Sidmouth Science Festival, an annual event founded in 2012. It has the support of a number of schools, community organisations, local businesses and churches, and its mission statement is to inform, educate and inspire all ages, especially the young. The 10 day event includes talks, demonstrations, interactive science trails in the Byes or seashore, quizzes, and competitions. The quality of scientific input has been enhanced considerably by the proximity of the national 'Met Centre' in Exeter and the Norman Lockyer Observatory. Separately from the Festival and throughout the year are monthly 'Café Scientifique' informal meetings in a coffee house when an expert talks for 20 minutes followed by discussion.

Café Scientifique glass blowing demonstration

The architect RW Sampson designed an astonishingly diverse style of buildings in Sidmouth including the Arcot Park council estate, Gliddons Toy Shop, Jubilee Terrace in All Saints Road and the imposing rather than attractive Victoria Hotel. Rock Cottage and the Unitarian Old Meeting were sensitively rebuilt. His Arts and Crafts style Edwardian villas in the Bickwell Valley are much sought after. It is appropriate, therefore, that a Sampson Society should be formed, in 2011, to appreciate his considerable accomplishments. It documents a comprehensive list of his properties and exercises a watching brief with regard to planning matters.

The 2008 financial crash and subsequent recession affected businesses in the town as it did nationwide. Nevertheless, there were few empty shops and the flagship stores, Fields and Potburys maintained business. The town has continued to attract many independent and high quality shops. Early in 2015 a brave or foolish, depending upon one's viewpoint, correspondent to the Sidmouth Herald said that she had recently moved to the town and suggested that there should be more chain stores to attract younger people and that many present shop owners were "lackadaisical". Subsequent letter columns in the Herald reflected the outrage and indignation of townspeople and such was the avalanche of replies that one could be forgiven for wondering whether the original letter had been an ingenious ploy of the Tourist Board.

It is however important not to be complacent. The 2006 Vision for Sidmouth proposal for a cultural centre at Port Royal, although widely supported, seems a very distant vision indeed. More specifically the SES Stationers in High Street became unoccupied in 2004. The large building, formerly the National Provincial Bank, was allowed to gradually deteriorate and parts of its façade crumbled, falling onto the pavement. Visitors were as surprised as residents that a town that takes such a pride in its heritage could tolerate for over a decade the gloomy, shabby appearance.

The 2011 census provided information that was largely expected. In a town of 12,569, almost 90% of the town population were born in England – the International School and Folk Week inject some welcome multiculturalism. Forty-eight per cent of the population are over 60 years of age, compared with a national average of 21%. Indeed the town has the highest elderly population in Devon, eclipsing Budleigh Salterton. Despite, or perhaps because of this age bias, Folk Week and the Science Festival are deliberately designed to attract young participants, and the Keith Owen Fund supports many youth projects. Furthermore sport is varied and flourishing in the town for all age groups with several new ventures this century. Sidmouth Rugby Club has new facilities in Sidford

The Cricket pavilion's new thatched roof

and its junior rugby section is one of the most popular and successful, for the size of the town, in the West Country. The Sidmouth Cricket Club has both an active colts section and a girls' squad. The cricket ground has, of course, one of the most beautiful seaside locations in the country. The Devon Minor County side stage both one-day and three-day matches during the season. The Association Football Club, known as the Vikings (derived from the Sidmouth coat of arms), has a growing club membership. Sidmouth and Ottery amalgamated their respective hockey clubs in 2012 and their thriving Junior Academy has links with primary and secondary schools in East Devon. Another fast growing interest is the town's Junior Surf Lifesaving Club which is aimed at making fitness fun and teaching youngsters how to read the sea and stay safe. The club had the added fillip of acquiring the lease to the ideal location of the Arches on the town front as their headquarters. The Sidmouth Sailing Club revived the annual Regatta in 1989 and the August event is a colourful highlight in the town's calendar. In 2009, the Sidmouth Gig Racing Club was formed and rows from the beach three times a week in the summer. Their two boats are named Alma and, appropriately, Keith Owen and both women's and men's teams compete in national championships in the Isles of Scilly.

Social historians of the English seaside town invariably refer to Sidmouth throughout its long history as 'exclusive'; their word rather than ours but perhaps a better word would be 'special'. In the first part of the present century, the town remains special but as this chapter describes it is, like the river that runs through it, in constant flux.

Alma

BIBLIOGRAPHY

Ankins, John; *Sidmouth: Yesterday's Shops*, Westprint 2011

Barnard, Rab & Christine; *The Knowle Sidmouth: A Stately Pleasure Dome; a house and its history*, Sid Vale Association 2013

Barnard, Christine & Rab*; A Case of Murder: Sidmouth and the Kent family*, Sid Vale Associaion 2013

Brownlee, Sylvia; *Sampson's Sidmouth*, Sid Vale Association 2009

Butler, Jeremy; *Peter Orlando Hutchinson's Travels in Victorian Devon: Illustrated Journals and sketchbooks 1846-1870*, Halsgrove 2000

Butler, Jeremy; *Peter Orlando Hutchinson's Diary of a Devon antiquary: Illustrated journals and sketchbooks 1871-1894*, Halsgrove 2010

Cornish, Vaughan; *Scenery of Sidmouth*, Cambridge University Press 1940

Creeke, Julia; *Life and Times in Sidmouth: A Guide to the Blue Plaques*, Sid Vale Association 2012

Creeke, Julia; *The Story of Sidmouth's Long Print*, Sid Vale Association 2013

Creeke, Julia; *Sidmouth's Long Print, "A Picture in Time"*, Sid Vale Association 2014

Creeke, Julia; *Salcombe Regis, An Anthology – 700 Years of Village Life*, The Friends of Salcombe Regis Parish Church 2015

Fung, Peter; *From Venus to Victoria: a history of Fortfield Terrace and Sidmouth 1790-1901*, Fortfield Publishing 2012

Golding, Brian; *Street Names of the Sid Valley*, Sidmouth Town Council 2011

Hardy, Christine; *Elizabeth Barrett-Browning: Sidmouth Letters and Poems 1832-5*, Sid Vale Association

Hyman, Nigel; *Sidmouth: People & Places*, Sid Vale Association 2014

Lane, Reg; *Old Sidmouth*, Devon Books Reprint 2001

Linehan, Catherine; *Peter Orlando Hutchinson of Sidmouth, Devon 1810-1897*, Sidmouth Museum 1989

Miles, Robert; *Sidmouth Scientists: Fellows of the Royal Society*, Sid Vale Association 2015

Reynolds, Stephen; *A Poor Man's House*, Halsgrove 7th edition 2001

Sutton, Anna; *A Story of Sidmouth*, James Townsend & Sons Exeter 1959

Trend, Roger; *Sidmouth Rocks: An introduction to Sidmouth's geology – or why are Sidmouth's rocks red?* Sid Vale Association 2013

Useful addresses:

Devon Heritage Centre (Devon Archives and Local Studies Service), Great Moor House, Bitten Road, Sowton, Exeter
www.devon.gov.uk/record_office

Sid Vale Association www.sidvaleassociation.org.uk

Sidmouth Museum, Hope Cottage, Church Street, Sidmouth EX10 8LY www.devonmuseums.net/Sidmouth-Museum/Devon-Museums

East Devon Area of Outstanding Natural Beauty
www.eastdevonaonb.org.uk

INDEX